50 Authentic Chinese Recipes for Home

By: Kelly Johnson

Table of Contents

- Mapo Tofu
- Kung Pao Chicken
- Sweet and Sour Pork
- Peking Duck
- Dumplings (Jiaozi)
- Hot and Sour Soup
- General Tso's Chicken
- Szechuan Beef
- Mongolian Beef
- Egg Fried Rice
- Chow Mein
- Spring Rolls
- Ma Po Eggplant
- Honey Walnut Shrimp
- Cantonese Roast Duck
- Dan Dan Noodles
- Dim Sum (Various varieties)
- Char Siu (Chinese BBQ Pork)
- Hainanese Chicken Rice
- Wonton Soup
- Beef and Broccoli
- Lo Mein
- Prawn Toast
- Gong Bao Shrimp
- Sweet Red Bean Paste Buns (Dou Sha Bao)
- Shanghai-Style Lion's Head Meatballs
- Cantonese Steamed Fish
- Three Cup Chicken (San Bei Ji)
- Salt and Pepper Squid
- Chinese Hot Pot
- Beef Chow Fun
- Ma La Xiang Guo (Spicy Numbing Stir-Fry)
- Scallion Pancakes
- Lion's Head Meatballs (Shi Zi Tou)
- Fish Fragrant Eggplant (Yu Xiang Qie Zi)

- Szechuan Hot and Sour Soup
- Shrimp Dumplings (Har Gow)
- Steamed Buns (Baozi)
- Stir-Fried Snow Peas with Garlic
- Crispy Duck Pancakes
- Taiwanese Beef Noodle Soup
- Chinese BBQ Ribs
- Eight Treasure Rice (Ba Bao Fan)
- Braised Pork Belly (Hong Shao Rou)
- Stir-Fried Green Beans with Minced Pork
- Clay Pot Rice (Bao Zai Fan)
- Zhajiangmian (Noodles with Soybean Paste)
- Crispy Shredded Beef
- Radish Cake (Luo Bo Gao)
- Egg Custard Tarts (Dan Ta)

Mapo Tofu

Ingredients:

- 400g firm tofu, cut into small cubes
- 100g minced pork or beef
- 2 tablespoons vegetable oil
- 2 cloves garlic, minced
- 1 tablespoon ginger, minced
- 2 green onions, chopped (separate white and green parts)
- 2 tablespoons doubanjiang (fermented broad bean paste)
- 1 tablespoon chili bean sauce (toban djan)
- 1 teaspoon Sichuan peppercorns, toasted and ground
- 1 tablespoon soy sauce
- 1 tablespoon Shaoxing wine (or dry sherry)
- 1 cup chicken or vegetable broth
- 1 teaspoon cornstarch mixed with 1 tablespoon water (slurry)
- Salt to taste
- Steamed rice, for serving
- Chopped green onions and cilantro, for garnish

Instructions:

1. Heat vegetable oil in a wok or large skillet over medium heat.
2. Add minced pork or beef to the wok. Stir-fry until browned and cooked through, breaking up any clumps with a spatula.
3. Push the meat to the side of the wok and add garlic, ginger, and the white parts of the green onions. Stir-fry for about 30 seconds until fragrant.
4. Add doubanjiang and chili bean sauce to the wok. Stir-fry for another minute until aromatic.
5. Add tofu cubes to the wok. Gently stir to combine with the meat and sauce, being careful not to break the tofu.
6. Pour in soy sauce, Shaoxing wine, and chicken or vegetable broth. Stir gently to combine.
7. Allow the mixture to simmer for about 5-7 minutes, stirring occasionally, until the tofu is heated through and the flavors meld together.
8. Add the Sichuan peppercorn powder and salt to taste. Stir to combine.

9. Stir in the cornstarch slurry to thicken the sauce. Cook for another minute until the sauce reaches your desired consistency.
10. Remove the wok from heat. Garnish with the green parts of the green onions and cilantro.
11. Serve hot with steamed rice.

Enjoy your homemade Mapo Tofu! Adjust the amount of chili bean sauce and Sichuan peppercorns according to your spice preference.

Kung Pao Chicken

Ingredients:

- 400g boneless, skinless chicken breasts or thighs, cut into bite-sized pieces
- 2 tablespoons vegetable oil
- 1/2 cup peanuts (preferably unsalted)
- 3-4 dried red chilies, seeded and cut into halves
- 3 cloves garlic, minced
- 1 tablespoon ginger, minced
- 2 green onions, chopped (separate white and green parts)
- 1 red bell pepper, diced
- 1/2 cup diced vegetables (optional, such as carrots or celery)
- 2 tablespoons soy sauce
- 1 tablespoon hoisin sauce
- 1 tablespoon Shaoxing wine (or dry sherry)
- 1 tablespoon rice vinegar
- 1 tablespoon sugar
- 1 teaspoon cornstarch mixed with 2 tablespoons water (slurry)
- Salt to taste
- Steamed rice, for serving

Instructions:

1. Heat vegetable oil in a wok or large skillet over high heat.
2. Add peanuts to the wok and stir-fry for about 1-2 minutes until lightly browned and fragrant. Remove from the wok and set aside.
3. In the same wok, add dried red chilies and stir-fry for about 30 seconds until aromatic. Be careful not to burn them.
4. Add minced garlic, ginger, and the white parts of the green onions to the wok. Stir-fry for another 30 seconds until fragrant.
5. Add diced chicken to the wok. Stir-fry until the chicken is cooked through and lightly browned.
6. Add diced bell pepper and any optional vegetables to the wok. Stir-fry for another 2-3 minutes until the vegetables are tender-crisp.
7. In a small bowl, mix together soy sauce, hoisin sauce, Shaoxing wine, rice vinegar, and sugar.

8. Pour the sauce mixture into the wok. Stir to combine with the chicken and vegetables.
9. Add the peanuts back to the wok. Stir to combine.
10. Stir in the cornstarch slurry to thicken the sauce. Cook for another minute until the sauce reaches your desired consistency.
11. Taste and adjust the seasoning with salt if needed.
12. Garnish with the green parts of the green onions.
13. Serve hot with steamed rice.

Enjoy your homemade Kung Pao Chicken! Adjust the amount of dried red chilies according to your spice preference.

Sweet and Sour Pork

Ingredients:

For the Pork:

- 400g pork loin or tenderloin, cut into bite-sized pieces
- 2 tablespoons soy sauce
- 1 tablespoon Shaoxing wine (or dry sherry)
- 1 egg, beaten
- 1/4 cup cornstarch
- Vegetable oil, for frying

For the Sweet and Sour Sauce:

- 1/4 cup ketchup
- 2 tablespoons rice vinegar
- 2 tablespoons brown sugar
- 1 tablespoon soy sauce
- 1 tablespoon cornstarch
- 1/2 cup pineapple chunks (fresh or canned)
- 1 bell pepper, cut into chunks
- 1 onion, cut into chunks
- 1 carrot, sliced (optional)
- 1 clove garlic, minced
- 1 teaspoon ginger, minced
- Vegetable oil, for stir-frying

Instructions:

1. In a bowl, marinate the pork pieces with soy sauce and Shaoxing wine for about 15-20 minutes.
2. In another bowl, mix together the beaten egg and cornstarch until smooth. Add the marinated pork pieces to the egg-cornstarch mixture and coat them well.
3. Heat vegetable oil in a deep frying pan or wok over medium-high heat. Fry the coated pork pieces in batches until they are golden brown and crispy. Remove them from the oil and drain on paper towels. Set aside.
4. In a small bowl, mix together ketchup, rice vinegar, brown sugar, soy sauce, and cornstarch to make the sweet and sour sauce. Set aside.

5. In the same pan or wok, heat a little vegetable oil over medium heat. Add minced garlic and ginger. Stir-fry for about 30 seconds until fragrant.
6. Add bell pepper, onion, and carrot (if using) to the pan. Stir-fry for about 2-3 minutes until the vegetables are tender-crisp.
7. Pour the sweet and sour sauce into the pan. Stir well to combine with the vegetables.
8. Add pineapple chunks to the pan. Stir gently to combine.
9. Allow the sauce to simmer for about 1-2 minutes until it thickens.
10. Add the fried pork pieces to the pan. Stir gently to coat them with the sauce.
11. Cook for another minute until the pork is heated through.
12. Taste and adjust the seasoning if needed.
13. Serve hot with steamed rice.

Enjoy your homemade Sweet and Sour Pork! Adjust the sweetness and sourness of the sauce according to your preference.

Peking Duck

Ingredients:

- 1 whole duck (about 4-5 pounds)
- 4 tablespoons honey
- 2 tablespoons soy sauce
- 1 tablespoon hoisin sauce
- 1 tablespoon rice vinegar
- 1 teaspoon Chinese five-spice powder
- 2 green onions, thinly sliced
- 1 cucumber, cut into thin matchsticks
- 12-16 small pancakes (store-bought or homemade)
- Hoisin sauce and/or plum sauce, for serving

Instructions:

1. Rinse the duck under cold water and pat dry with paper towels. Remove any excess fat from the cavity.
2. In a small bowl, mix together honey, soy sauce, hoisin sauce, rice vinegar, and Chinese five-spice powder to make the marinade.
3. Brush the marinade all over the duck, inside and out. Make sure to coat the duck evenly.
4. Place the duck on a rack in a roasting pan, breast side up. Refrigerate uncovered for at least 6 hours or overnight to allow the skin to dry out.
5. Preheat the oven to 350°F (175°C). Roast the duck in the preheated oven for about 2-2.5 hours, or until the skin is golden brown and crispy, and the internal temperature reaches 165°F (75°C).
6. Remove the duck from the oven and let it rest for about 10 minutes before carving.
7. To serve, slice the duck into thin pieces, including both meat and skin.
8. Arrange the sliced duck on a platter with the green onions and cucumber matchsticks.
9. Serve the duck with small pancakes, hoisin sauce, and/or plum sauce for dipping.
10. To eat, place a slice of duck, some green onions and cucumber, and a dollop of sauce on a pancake. Roll up the pancake and enjoy!

Enjoy your homemade Peking Duck! Adjust the seasoning and cooking time according to your preference and the size of the duck.

Dumplings (Jiaozi)

Ingredients:

For the dough:

- 2 cups all-purpose flour
- 3/4 cup cold water

For the filling:

- 300g ground pork
- 1 cup finely chopped cabbage
- 2 green onions, finely chopped
- 2 tablespoons soy sauce
- 1 tablespoon sesame oil
- 1 tablespoon rice vinegar
- 1 teaspoon grated ginger
- 2 cloves garlic, minced
- Salt and pepper to taste

For dipping sauce:

- 2 tablespoons soy sauce
- 1 tablespoon rice vinegar
- 1 teaspoon sesame oil
- 1 teaspoon grated ginger
- 1 teaspoon chili oil (optional)
- Chopped green onions for garnish (optional)

Instructions:

1. Start by making the dough. In a large mixing bowl, combine the flour and cold water. Mix until a dough forms.
2. Knead the dough on a floured surface for about 5-7 minutes until smooth and elastic. Cover with a damp cloth and let it rest for 30 minutes.

3. While the dough is resting, prepare the filling. In a large bowl, combine ground pork, chopped cabbage, green onions, soy sauce, sesame oil, rice vinegar, grated ginger, minced garlic, salt, and pepper. Mix until well combined.
4. After the dough has rested, divide it into small pieces. Roll each piece into a thin circle, about 3 inches in diameter.
5. Place a spoonful of filling in the center of each dough circle.
6. Fold the dough over the filling to create a half-moon shape. Press the edges firmly to seal, pleating the dough if desired.
7. Repeat with the remaining dough and filling until all the dumplings are assembled.
8. To cook the dumplings, you can either boil, steam, or pan-fry them.
    - To boil: Bring a large pot of water to a boil. Carefully drop the dumplings into the boiling water and cook until they float to the surface, about 3-5 minutes.
    - To steam: Arrange the dumplings on a steamer basket lined with parchment paper or cabbage leaves. Steam for about 10-12 minutes until cooked through.
    - To pan-fry (potstickers): Heat some oil in a non-stick skillet over medium heat. Place the dumplings in the skillet, flat side down. Cook until the bottoms are golden brown, then add water to the skillet and cover with a lid. Steam until the water has evaporated and the dumplings are cooked through.
9. While the dumplings are cooking, prepare the dipping sauce. In a small bowl, mix together soy sauce, rice vinegar, sesame oil, grated ginger, and chili oil if using.
10. Serve the cooked dumplings hot with the dipping sauce on the side. Garnish with chopped green onions if desired.

Enjoy your homemade Jiaozi! Adjust the filling ingredients and cooking method according to your preference.

Hot and Sour Soup

Ingredients:

- 6 cups chicken or vegetable broth
- 200g firm tofu, cut into small cubes
- 100g shiitake mushrooms, thinly sliced
- 1/2 cup bamboo shoots, thinly sliced
- 1/4 cup rice vinegar
- 3 tablespoons soy sauce
- 2 tablespoons cornstarch
- 2 eggs, beaten
- 2 green onions, thinly sliced
- 1 tablespoon grated ginger
- 2 cloves garlic, minced
- 1 teaspoon sesame oil
- 1 teaspoon chili oil (optional)
- Salt and white pepper to taste
- Chopped cilantro for garnish (optional)

Instructions:

1. In a large pot, bring the chicken or vegetable broth to a simmer over medium heat.
2. Add tofu cubes, sliced shiitake mushrooms, and bamboo shoots to the pot. Simmer for about 5-7 minutes until the mushrooms are tender.
3. In a small bowl, whisk together rice vinegar, soy sauce, and cornstarch until smooth.
4. Slowly pour the vinegar mixture into the soup, stirring constantly. Allow the soup to simmer for another 2-3 minutes until slightly thickened.
5. While stirring the soup in a circular motion, slowly pour the beaten eggs into the pot in a steady stream. The eggs will cook and form ribbons in the soup.
6. Add thinly sliced green onions, grated ginger, minced garlic, sesame oil, and chili oil (if using) to the pot. Stir to combine.
7. Taste the soup and adjust the seasoning with salt and white pepper as needed.
8. Ladle the hot and sour soup into serving bowls. Garnish with chopped cilantro if desired.
9. Serve hot as an appetizer or alongside steamed rice for a light meal.

Enjoy your homemade Hot and Sour Soup! Adjust the amount of vinegar and chili oil according to your preference for sourness and spiciness.

General Tso's Chicken

Ingredients:

For the chicken:

- 500g boneless, skinless chicken thighs or breasts, cut into bite-sized pieces
- 1 egg
- 1/2 cup cornstarch
- Vegetable oil, for frying

For the sauce:

- 1/4 cup soy sauce
- 2 tablespoons hoisin sauce
- 2 tablespoons rice vinegar
- 2 tablespoons brown sugar
- 1 tablespoon cornstarch
- 1 teaspoon sesame oil
- 2 cloves garlic, minced
- 1 teaspoon grated ginger
- 2 dried red chilies (optional)
- 2 green onions, chopped (for garnish)
- Toasted sesame seeds (for garnish)

Instructions:

1. In a bowl, whisk the egg. Dip the chicken pieces into the egg, making sure they are well coated.
2. Place the cornstarch in a shallow dish. Dredge each egg-coated chicken piece in the cornstarch, shaking off any excess.
3. Heat vegetable oil in a deep frying pan or wok over medium-high heat. Fry the coated chicken pieces in batches until they are golden brown and crispy. Remove them from the oil and drain on paper towels. Set aside.
4. In a small bowl, mix together soy sauce, hoisin sauce, rice vinegar, brown sugar, cornstarch, sesame oil, minced garlic, and grated ginger to make the sauce. Set aside.
5. In a clean wok or large skillet, heat a little vegetable oil over medium heat. Add dried red chilies if using, and stir-fry for about 30 seconds until fragrant.

6. Add the sauce mixture to the wok. Cook, stirring constantly, until the sauce thickens and becomes glossy, about 2-3 minutes.
7. Add the fried chicken pieces to the wok. Stir to coat them evenly with the sauce.
8. Continue to cook for another minute until the chicken is heated through and the sauce clings to the chicken.
9. Remove the wok from heat. Transfer the General Tso's Chicken to a serving plate.
10. Garnish with chopped green onions and toasted sesame seeds.
11. Serve hot with steamed rice.

Enjoy your homemade General Tso's Chicken! Adjust the amount of dried red chilies according to your spice preference.

Szechuan Beef

Ingredients:

For the marinade:

- 500g beef steak (flank steak or sirloin), thinly sliced against the grain
- 2 tablespoons soy sauce
- 1 tablespoon Shaoxing wine (or dry sherry)
- 1 tablespoon cornstarch

For the sauce:

- 3 tablespoons soy sauce
- 2 tablespoons hoisin sauce
- 2 tablespoons rice vinegar
- 1 tablespoon sugar
- 1 tablespoon sesame oil
- 2 cloves garlic, minced
- 1 tablespoon grated ginger
- 1-2 tablespoons Szechuan peppercorns, crushed (adjust to taste)
- 2 dried red chilies, chopped (adjust to taste)
- 1 tablespoon cornstarch mixed with 2 tablespoons water (slurry)

For stir-frying:

- 2 tablespoons vegetable oil
- 1 bell pepper, thinly sliced
- 1 onion, thinly sliced
- 2 green onions, chopped (for garnish)
- Cooked rice, for serving

Instructions:

1. In a bowl, combine thinly sliced beef with soy sauce, Shaoxing wine, and cornstarch. Mix well to coat the beef evenly. Let it marinate for about 15-20 minutes.

2. In another bowl, mix together soy sauce, hoisin sauce, rice vinegar, sugar, sesame oil, minced garlic, grated ginger, crushed Szechuan peppercorns, and chopped dried red chilies to make the sauce. Set aside.
3. Heat vegetable oil in a wok or large skillet over high heat.
4. Add the marinated beef to the wok in a single layer. Stir-fry for 2-3 minutes until the beef is browned but still slightly pink in the center. Remove the beef from the wok and set aside.
5. In the same wok, add a little more oil if needed. Add thinly sliced bell pepper and onion to the wok. Stir-fry for 2-3 minutes until the vegetables are tender-crisp.
6. Return the cooked beef to the wok. Stir to combine with the vegetables.
7. Pour the sauce mixture into the wok. Stir well to coat the beef and vegetables.
8. Stir in the cornstarch slurry to thicken the sauce. Cook for another minute until the sauce reaches your desired consistency.
9. Taste and adjust the seasoning if needed.
10. Remove the wok from heat. Transfer the Szechuan Beef to a serving plate.
11. Garnish with chopped green onions.
12. Serve hot with steamed rice.

Enjoy your homemade Szechuan Beef! Adjust the amount of Szechuan peppercorns and dried red chilies according to your spice preference.

Mongolian Beef

Ingredients:

For the beef:

- 500g beef steak (flank steak or sirloin), thinly sliced against the grain
- 2 tablespoons cornstarch
- 2 tablespoons vegetable oil
- 2 cloves garlic, minced
- 1 tablespoon grated ginger
- 2 green onions, chopped (separate white and green parts)

For the sauce:

- 1/4 cup soy sauce
- 1/4 cup water
- 2 tablespoons hoisin sauce
- 2 tablespoons brown sugar
- 1 tablespoon rice vinegar
- 1 teaspoon sesame oil
- 1 tablespoon cornstarch

Instructions:

1. In a bowl, toss the thinly sliced beef with cornstarch until evenly coated. Set aside.
2. In a separate bowl, mix together soy sauce, water, hoisin sauce, brown sugar, rice vinegar, sesame oil, and cornstarch to make the sauce. Set aside.
3. Heat vegetable oil in a wok or large skillet over high heat.
4. Add minced garlic, grated ginger, and the white parts of the green onions to the wok. Stir-fry for about 30 seconds until fragrant.
5. Add the beef to the wok in a single layer. Stir-fry for 2-3 minutes until browned but still slightly pink in the center. Remove the beef from the wok and set aside.
6. In the same wok, pour the sauce mixture. Cook, stirring constantly, until the sauce thickens and becomes glossy, about 2-3 minutes.
7. Return the cooked beef to the wok. Stir to coat the beef evenly with the sauce.
8. Continue to cook for another minute until the beef is heated through and the sauce clings to the beef.

9. Remove the wok from heat. Transfer the Mongolian Beef to a serving plate.
10. Garnish with chopped green onions.
11. Serve hot with steamed rice.

Enjoy your homemade Mongolian Beef! Adjust the amount of brown sugar and soy sauce according to your taste preference.

Egg Fried Rice

Ingredients:

- 3 cups cooked rice (preferably cold, leftover rice)
- 2 eggs, lightly beaten
- 2 tablespoons vegetable oil
- 2 cloves garlic, minced
- 1 small onion, finely chopped
- 1 cup mixed vegetables (such as carrots, peas, and corn)
- 2 tablespoons soy sauce
- 1 tablespoon oyster sauce (optional)
- Salt and pepper to taste
- Chopped green onions for garnish (optional)
- Sesame oil for drizzling (optional)

Instructions:

1. Heat vegetable oil in a large skillet or wok over medium heat.
2. Add minced garlic and chopped onion to the skillet. Stir-fry for about 1-2 minutes until the onion is translucent and fragrant.
3. Push the onion and garlic to one side of the skillet. Pour the beaten eggs into the empty side of the skillet. Allow them to cook for a few seconds until partially set.
4. Use a spatula to scramble the eggs, breaking them into small pieces as they cook.
5. Add the mixed vegetables to the skillet. Stir-fry for another 2-3 minutes until the vegetables are tender.
6. Add the cooked rice to the skillet. Break up any clumps and stir to combine with the vegetables and eggs.
7. Pour soy sauce and oyster sauce (if using) over the rice. Stir well to evenly distribute the sauces.
8. Continue to stir-fry for another 3-4 minutes until the rice is heated through and slightly crispy.
9. Taste the fried rice and adjust the seasoning with salt and pepper if needed.
10. Remove the skillet from heat. Transfer the Egg Fried Rice to a serving dish.
11. Garnish with chopped green onions and drizzle with sesame oil if desired.
12. Serve hot as a delicious main dish or side dish.

Enjoy your homemade Egg Fried Rice! You can customize this recipe by adding your favorite protein, such as cooked chicken, shrimp, or tofu. Feel free to adjust the amount of soy sauce and vegetables according to your taste preference.

Chow Mein

Ingredients:

- 200g chow mein noodles (or egg noodles)
- 2 tablespoons vegetable oil
- 2 boneless, skinless chicken breasts, thinly sliced
- 2 cloves garlic, minced
- 1 small onion, thinly sliced
- 1 bell pepper, thinly sliced
- 1 cup shredded cabbage
- 1 cup bean sprouts
- 2 green onions, chopped (separate white and green parts)
- 2 tablespoons soy sauce
- 1 tablespoon oyster sauce
- 1 teaspoon sesame oil
- Salt and pepper to taste

Instructions:

1. Cook the chow mein noodles according to the package instructions until al dente. Drain and set aside.
2. In a large skillet or wok, heat vegetable oil over medium-high heat.
3. Add thinly sliced chicken breast to the skillet. Stir-fry for 3-4 minutes until browned and cooked through. Remove the chicken from the skillet and set aside.
4. In the same skillet, add minced garlic and thinly sliced onion. Stir-fry for about 1-2 minutes until fragrant and softened.
5. Add thinly sliced bell pepper, shredded cabbage, bean sprouts, and the white parts of the green onions to the skillet. Stir-fry for another 2-3 minutes until the vegetables are tender-crisp.
6. Return the cooked chicken to the skillet. Stir to combine with the vegetables.
7. Add cooked chow mein noodles to the skillet. Toss everything together.
8. Pour soy sauce, oyster sauce, and sesame oil over the noodles and chicken. Stir well to coat everything evenly.
9. Continue to stir-fry for another 2-3 minutes until everything is heated through and well combined.
10. Taste the chow mein and adjust the seasoning with salt and pepper if needed.
11. Remove the skillet from heat. Transfer the Chicken Chow Mein to a serving dish.
12. Garnish with chopped green onions (green parts).

13. Serve hot as a delicious main dish.

Enjoy your homemade Chicken Chow Mein! Feel free to customize this recipe by adding your favorite vegetables or protein.

Spring Rolls

Ingredients:

For the filling:

- 2 tablespoons vegetable oil
- 2 cloves garlic, minced
- 1 small onion, finely chopped
- 1 cup shredded cabbage
- 1 carrot, julienned
- 1 bell pepper, thinly sliced
- 1 cup bean sprouts
- 1/2 cup sliced mushrooms (optional)
- 2 tablespoons soy sauce
- 1 tablespoon oyster sauce (optional)
- 1 teaspoon sesame oil
- Salt and pepper to taste
- 12-15 spring roll wrappers
- 1 egg, beaten (for sealing the wrappers)
- Vegetable oil for frying
- Sweet chili sauce or plum sauce for dipping

Instructions:

1. Heat vegetable oil in a large skillet or wok over medium-high heat.
2. Add minced garlic and finely chopped onion to the skillet. Stir-fry for about 1-2 minutes until fragrant and softened.
3. Add shredded cabbage, julienned carrot, thinly sliced bell pepper, bean sprouts, and sliced mushrooms (if using) to the skillet. Stir-fry for another 3-4 minutes until the vegetables are tender-crisp.
4. Pour soy sauce, oyster sauce (if using), and sesame oil over the vegetables. Stir well to coat everything evenly.
5. Continue to stir-fry for another 1-2 minutes. Taste the filling and adjust the seasoning with salt and pepper if needed. Remove the skillet from heat and let the filling cool slightly.
6. Place a spring roll wrapper on a clean, flat surface. Spoon about 2-3 tablespoons of the vegetable filling onto the bottom third of the wrapper.

7. Fold the bottom edge of the wrapper over the filling, then fold in the sides, and roll it up tightly into a cylinder shape, making sure the edges are sealed.
8. Brush a little beaten egg along the top edge of the wrapper to seal it completely.
9. Repeat with the remaining wrappers and filling until all the spring rolls are assembled.
10. Heat vegetable oil in a deep fryer or large skillet to 350°F (175°C).
11. Carefully place the spring rolls in the hot oil, a few at a time, seam side down. Fry for about 2-3 minutes on each side until they are golden brown and crispy.
12. Remove the fried spring rolls from the oil and drain on paper towels.
13. Serve hot with sweet chili sauce or plum sauce for dipping.

Enjoy your homemade Vegetable Spring Rolls! You can also add cooked shrimp, chicken, or tofu to the filling if desired.

Ma Po Eggplant

Ingredients:

- 2 medium-sized Chinese eggplants, cut into bite-sized pieces
- 2 tablespoons vegetable oil
- 2 cloves garlic, minced
- 1 tablespoon grated ginger
- 2 green onions, chopped (separate white and green parts)
- 200g ground pork (optional, can be omitted for a vegetarian version)
- 2 tablespoons doubanjiang (spicy bean paste)
- 1 tablespoon soy sauce
- 1 tablespoon Shaoxing wine (or dry sherry)
- 1 teaspoon sugar
- 1 cup vegetable or chicken broth
- 1 teaspoon cornstarch mixed with 2 tablespoons water (slurry)
- 1 teaspoon sesame oil
- Cooked rice, for serving

Instructions:

1. Heat vegetable oil in a wok or large skillet over medium heat.
2. Add minced garlic, grated ginger, and the white parts of the green onions to the wok. Stir-fry for about 30 seconds until fragrant.
3. If using ground pork, add it to the wok. Stir-fry until the pork is browned and cooked through.
4. Add doubanjiang (spicy bean paste) to the wok. Stir-fry for another minute to release its flavor.
5. Add the chopped eggplant to the wok. Stir-fry for 2-3 minutes until the eggplant starts to soften.
6. Pour soy sauce, Shaoxing wine, and sugar over the eggplant. Stir to coat evenly.
7. Pour vegetable or chicken broth into the wok. Bring to a simmer and cook for 5-7 minutes until the eggplant is tender.
8. Stir in the cornstarch slurry to thicken the sauce. Cook for another minute until the sauce reaches your desired consistency.
9. Taste the Ma Po Eggplant and adjust the seasoning if needed.
10. Remove the wok from heat. Drizzle sesame oil over the Ma Po Eggplant and sprinkle with the green parts of the chopped green onions.

11. Serve hot with steamed rice.

Enjoy your homemade Ma Po Eggplant! Adjust the amount of doubanjiang according to your spice preference. You can also add diced tofu for a vegetarian version or top with chopped peanuts or cilantro for extra flavor.

Honey Walnut Shrimp

Ingredients:

For the shrimp:

- 500g large shrimp, peeled and deveined
- Salt and pepper to taste
- 1 egg white
- 1/2 cup cornstarch
- Vegetable oil for frying

For the honey walnut glaze:

- 1/2 cup walnuts
- 1/4 cup mayonnaise
- 2 tablespoons honey
- 1 tablespoon sweetened condensed milk
- 1 tablespoon lemon juice
- 1/4 teaspoon salt

Instructions:

1. Season the peeled and deveined shrimp with salt and pepper.
2. In a bowl, whisk the egg white until frothy. Dip each shrimp into the egg white, then dredge in cornstarch to coat evenly.
3. Heat vegetable oil in a deep fryer or large skillet to 350°F (175°C). Fry the coated shrimp in batches for about 2-3 minutes until golden brown and crispy. Remove from the oil and drain on paper towels. Set aside.
4. Toast the walnuts in a dry skillet over medium heat for 2-3 minutes until fragrant. Remove from heat and set aside.
5. In a small bowl, mix together mayonnaise, honey, sweetened condensed milk, lemon juice, and salt to make the honey walnut glaze.
6. In a separate skillet, heat the honey walnut glaze over medium heat. Add the fried shrimp and toasted walnuts to the skillet. Toss until the shrimp and walnuts are evenly coated with the glaze.
7. Cook for another minute until the glaze thickens slightly and coats the shrimp and walnuts.
8. Remove from heat and transfer the Honey Walnut Shrimp to a serving plate.

9. Serve hot as a delicious appetizer or main dish.

Enjoy your homemade Honey Walnut Shrimp! Adjust the sweetness of the glaze according to your taste preference. You can also garnish with sesame seeds or chopped green onions for extra flavor.

Cantonese Roast Duck

Ingredients:

- 1 whole duck (about 4-5 pounds)
- 2 tablespoons maltose or honey
- 2 tablespoons soy sauce
- 2 tablespoons hoisin sauce
- 1 tablespoon Shaoxing wine (or dry sherry)
- 1 teaspoon five-spice powder
- 1 teaspoon sesame oil
- 2 cloves garlic, minced
- 1-inch piece of ginger, sliced
- Salt, to taste
- Optional: 1 tablespoon rice vinegar (for brushing)

Instructions:

1. Rinse the duck inside and out under cold water. Pat dry with paper towels.
2. In a small bowl, mix together maltose (or honey), soy sauce, hoisin sauce, Shaoxing wine, five-spice powder, sesame oil, minced garlic, and sliced ginger to make the marinade.
3. Rub the marinade all over the duck, inside and out, making sure it's well coated. Place the sliced ginger inside the cavity of the duck. Sprinkle a little salt over the skin.
4. Let the duck marinate in the refrigerator, uncovered, for at least 4 hours or overnight for best results.
5. Preheat the oven to 375°F (190°C).
6. Place the marinated duck on a rack in a roasting pan, breast side up.
7. Roast the duck in the preheated oven for about 1.5 to 2 hours, depending on the size of the duck, or until the skin is golden brown and crispy, and the internal temperature reaches 165°F (75°C).
8. Optional: About halfway through the roasting time, you can brush the duck with rice vinegar mixed with a little water to enhance the color and add a tangy flavor.
9. Once cooked, remove the duck from the oven and let it rest for about 10-15 minutes before carving.
10. Carve the duck into serving pieces, such as thighs, legs, wings, and breast meat.
11. Serve hot with steamed rice and your favorite dipping sauce, such as hoisin sauce or plum sauce.

Enjoy your homemade Cantonese Roast Duck! Adjust the seasoning and cooking time according to your preference and the size of the duck.

Dan Dan Noodles

Ingredients:

For the noodles:

- 200g fresh or dried Chinese egg noodles
- 2 tablespoons vegetable oil

For the sauce:

- 2 tablespoons sesame paste (tahini)
- 2 tablespoons soy sauce
- 1 tablespoon Chinese black vinegar (or substitute with rice vinegar)
- 1 tablespoon chili oil (adjust to taste)
- 1 tablespoon sugar
- 1 clove garlic, minced
- 1 teaspoon grated ginger
- 1/4 cup chicken or vegetable broth
- Salt, to taste

For the topping:

- 200g ground pork (optional)
- 2 tablespoons vegetable oil
- 2 cloves garlic, minced
- 1 tablespoon grated ginger
- 2 green onions, chopped (separate white and green parts)
- 2 tablespoons soy sauce
- 1 tablespoon Shaoxing wine (or dry sherry)
- 1 teaspoon cornstarch mixed with 2 tablespoons water (slurry)
- Chopped peanuts, for garnish (optional)
- Chopped cilantro, for garnish (optional)

Instructions:

1. Cook the Chinese egg noodles according to the package instructions until al dente. Drain and rinse under cold water to stop the cooking process. Toss with 2 tablespoons of vegetable oil to prevent sticking. Set aside.
2. In a small bowl, mix together sesame paste, soy sauce, Chinese black vinegar, chili oil, sugar, minced garlic, grated ginger, and chicken or vegetable broth to make the sauce. Adjust the seasoning to taste, adding salt if needed. Set aside.
3. If using ground pork, heat 2 tablespoons of vegetable oil in a skillet over medium-high heat. Add minced garlic, grated ginger, and the white parts of the chopped green onions. Stir-fry for about 1 minute until fragrant.
4. Add the ground pork to the skillet. Stir-fry until browned and cooked through.
5. Pour soy sauce and Shaoxing wine (or dry sherry) over the pork. Stir to combine.
6. Pour the cornstarch slurry into the skillet. Stir well to thicken the sauce. Cook for another minute until the sauce coats the pork evenly. Remove from heat.
7. To assemble the Dan Dan Noodles, divide the cooked noodles among serving bowls.
8. Pour the prepared sauce over the noodles, dividing it evenly among the bowls.
9. Top each bowl of noodles with the cooked ground pork mixture.
10. Garnish with chopped peanuts, chopped cilantro, and the green parts of the chopped green onions, if desired.
11. Serve immediately and enjoy!

Enjoy your homemade Dan Dan Noodles! Adjust the level of spiciness according to your preference by increasing or decreasing the amount of chili oil.

Dim Sum (Various varieties)

Ingredients:

- 250g ground pork
- 100g shrimp, peeled, deveined, and chopped
- 2 tablespoons soy sauce
- 1 tablespoon oyster sauce
- 1 tablespoon sesame oil
- 1 tablespoon cornstarch
- 1 tablespoon sugar
- 1 teaspoon grated ginger
- 1 teaspoon minced garlic
- 1/4 cup chopped green onions
- 24 round dumpling wrappers
- 24 small round pieces of carrot or pea for garnish (optional)

Instructions:

1. In a bowl, mix together ground pork, chopped shrimp, soy sauce, oyster sauce, sesame oil, cornstarch, sugar, ginger, garlic, and green onions until well combined.
2. Place a spoonful of the pork mixture in the center of each dumpling wrapper. Gather the edges and twist to seal, leaving the top open. Optionally, place a piece of carrot or pea on top for garnish.
3. Place the dumplings in a steamer lined with parchment paper. Steam for about 10-12 minutes until cooked through.

Char Siu Bao (Barbecue Pork Buns)

Ingredients:

- 1 cup diced char siu (barbecue pork)
- 1 tablespoon vegetable oil
- 1/4 cup finely chopped onion
- 1 clove garlic, minced
- 2 tablespoons hoisin sauce
- 1 tablespoon soy sauce
- 1 tablespoon oyster sauce
- 1 tablespoon sugar
- 1 teaspoon sesame oil
- 12 round bun wrappers

Instructions:

1. Heat oil in a skillet over medium heat. Add onion and garlic, sauté until fragrant.
2. Add diced char siu, hoisin sauce, soy sauce, oyster sauce, sugar, and sesame oil. Cook until heated through and well combined. Let cool.
3. Place a spoonful of the char siu mixture in the center of each bun wrapper. Gather the edges and twist to seal.
4. Place the buns on squares of parchment paper and steam for about 15-20 minutes until puffed and cooked through.

Ha Gow (Shrimp Dumplings)

Ingredients:

- 200g shrimp, peeled and deveined
- 1 tablespoon soy sauce
- 1 teaspoon sesame oil
- 1/2 teaspoon sugar
- Pinch of white pepper
- 1/4 cup bamboo shoots, finely chopped
- 1 tablespoon cornstarch
- 12 round dumpling wrappers

Instructions:

1. Chop the shrimp into small pieces. In a bowl, mix shrimp with soy sauce, sesame oil, sugar, white pepper, and bamboo shoots. Add cornstarch and mix until well combined.
2. Place a spoonful of the shrimp mixture in the center of each dumpling wrapper. Moisten the edges with water and fold the wrapper over the filling, pleating the edges to seal.
3. Place the dumplings in a bamboo steamer lined with parchment paper. Steam for about 8-10 minutes until the shrimp is cooked through and the wrappers are translucent.

These recipes should help you create a delicious dim sum feast at home! Adjust seasonings and ingredients to your taste preference. Enjoy!

Char Siu (Chinese BBQ Pork)

Ingredients:

- 500g pork shoulder or pork belly, cut into thin strips or slices
- 2 cloves garlic, minced
- 2 tablespoons honey
- 2 tablespoons hoisin sauce
- 2 tablespoons soy sauce
- 1 tablespoon oyster sauce
- 1 tablespoon Shaoxing wine (or dry sherry)
- 1 tablespoon sesame oil
- 1 teaspoon five-spice powder
- 1/2 teaspoon white pepper
- Red food coloring (optional, for traditional color)
- Sliced green onions and sesame seeds for garnish (optional)

Instructions:

1. In a bowl, mix together minced garlic, honey, hoisin sauce, soy sauce, oyster sauce, Shaoxing wine, sesame oil, five-spice powder, and white pepper. If using, add a few drops of red food coloring to achieve the traditional char siu color.
2. Add the pork strips to the marinade and mix well, ensuring all pieces are coated. Cover and refrigerate for at least 4 hours, or preferably overnight, to allow the flavors to meld.
3. Preheat the oven to 180°C (350°F).
4. Remove the marinated pork from the refrigerator and let it come to room temperature.
5. Thread the pork strips onto skewers or place them on a wire rack set over a baking tray to catch drips.
6. Bake in the preheated oven for about 25-30 minutes, turning halfway through, until the pork is cooked through and caramelized on the edges.
7. If desired, broil the pork for an additional 2-3 minutes at the end to achieve a deeper caramelization.
8. Remove the char siu from the oven and let it rest for a few minutes before slicing.
9. Garnish with sliced green onions and sesame seeds, if desired.
10. Serve the char siu hot with steamed rice or noodles, or use it as a filling for buns or stir-fries.

Enjoy your homemade Char Siu! Adjust the seasoning and cooking time according to your taste preference and the thickness of the pork slices.

Hainanese Chicken Rice

Ingredients:

For the Chicken:

- 1 whole chicken (about 1.5 kg)
- 2 spring onions (scallions), white parts only
- 3 slices ginger
- Salt, to taste
- Ice water (for cooling)

For the Rice:

- 2 cups jasmine rice
- 3 cups chicken broth (from cooking the chicken)
- 3 slices ginger
- 2 cloves garlic, minced
- Salt, to taste

For the Dipping Sauce:

- 3 tablespoons soy sauce
- 2 tablespoons sesame oil
- 2 tablespoons finely chopped ginger
- 2 tablespoons finely chopped garlic
- 2 tablespoons chopped spring onions (scallions)
- Chili sauce (optional)

For Garnish:

- Fresh cucumber slices
- Fresh cilantro (coriander) leaves

Instructions:

Cooking the Chicken:

1. Rinse the chicken under cold water, inside and out. Remove any excess fat and pat dry with paper towels.
2. Stuff the cavity of the chicken with spring onion and ginger slices.
3. In a large pot, bring water to a boil. Add a pinch of salt.

4. Gently lower the chicken into the boiling water, breast-side down. Bring the water back to a gentle simmer.
5. Cover the pot and let the chicken simmer for about 30-40 minutes, or until cooked through. The internal temperature of the chicken should reach 75°C (165°F).
6. Once cooked, carefully remove the chicken from the pot and immediately submerge it in ice water to stop the cooking process and to give the skin a firm texture. Let it cool for about 20 minutes.

Cooking the Rice:

1. Rinse the jasmine rice under cold water until the water runs clear. Drain well.
2. In a saucepan, heat a little oil over medium heat. Add minced garlic and ginger slices. Sauté until fragrant.
3. Add the drained rice to the saucepan and stir to coat with the aromatics.
4. Transfer the rice to a rice cooker. Add chicken broth (from cooking the chicken) instead of water, following the rice cooker's instructions for the water-to-rice ratio.
5. Cook the rice according to the rice cooker's instructions.

Making the Dipping Sauce:

1. In a small bowl, mix together soy sauce, sesame oil, chopped ginger, chopped garlic, and chopped spring onions. Add chili sauce if desired. Adjust seasoning to taste.

Serving:

1. Once the chicken has cooled, remove and discard the spring onion and ginger stuffing from the cavity.
2. Cut the chicken into serving pieces.
3. Serve the chicken with the fragrant rice, cucumber slices, fresh cilantro leaves, and dipping sauce on the side.
4. Enjoy your delicious Hainanese Chicken Rice!

This dish is traditionally served warm, but you can also enjoy it at room temperature.

Adjust the seasoning and spice level of the dipping sauce according to your taste preference.

Wonton Soup

Ingredients:

For the Wontons:

- 250g ground pork
- 150g peeled and deveined shrimp, chopped
- 2 cloves garlic, minced
- 1 tablespoon soy sauce
- 1 tablespoon oyster sauce
- 1 teaspoon sesame oil
- 1 teaspoon grated ginger
- 1/4 cup chopped green onions
- 1/4 teaspoon white pepper
- 24 square wonton wrappers

For the Soup:

- 4 cups chicken broth
- 2 cups water
- 2 slices ginger
- 2 cloves garlic, smashed
- 1 tablespoon soy sauce
- 1 tablespoon oyster sauce
- 1 teaspoon sesame oil
- Salt and pepper, to taste
- Chopped green onions, for garnish
- Sliced fresh cilantro (optional)

Instructions:

Making the Wontons:

1. In a large bowl, combine ground pork, chopped shrimp, minced garlic, soy sauce, oyster sauce, sesame oil, grated ginger, chopped green onions, and white pepper. Mix well until evenly combined.
2. Place a small spoonful of the filling in the center of each wonton wrapper. Moisten the edges with water and fold the wrapper diagonally to form a triangle, pressing the edges to seal. Bring the two corners together and overlap slightly, moisten with water, and press to seal.

3. Repeat with the remaining filling and wrappers until all the filling is used up. You should have about 24 wontons.

Making the Soup:

1. In a large pot, combine chicken broth, water, sliced ginger, smashed garlic, soy sauce, oyster sauce, and sesame oil. Bring to a boil over medium-high heat.
2. Once the soup is boiling, carefully add the wontons one by one, stirring gently to prevent sticking. Let the soup return to a boil.
3. Reduce the heat to medium-low and let the soup simmer for about 5-7 minutes, or until the wontons are cooked through and float to the surface.
4. Season the soup with salt and pepper to taste.
5. Ladle the hot soup into bowls, making sure to distribute the wontons evenly. Garnish with chopped green onions and sliced fresh cilantro, if desired.
6. Serve hot and enjoy your delicious homemade Wonton Soup!

Feel free to customize the soup by adding your favorite vegetables such as bok choy, spinach, or sliced mushrooms. Adjust the seasoning according to your taste preference.

Beef and Broccoli

Ingredients:

For the Beef Marinade:

- 400g beef steak (flank steak or sirloin), thinly sliced against the grain
- 2 tablespoons soy sauce
- 1 tablespoon oyster sauce
- 1 tablespoon cornstarch
- 1 teaspoon sesame oil
- 1 teaspoon sugar
- 1/2 teaspoon black pepper

For the Stir-Fry:

- 2 tablespoons vegetable oil
- 3 cloves garlic, minced
- 1 teaspoon grated ginger
- 1 head broccoli, cut into florets
- 1/2 cup beef broth or water
- 2 tablespoons oyster sauce
- 1 tablespoon soy sauce
- 1 tablespoon hoisin sauce
- 1 teaspoon cornstarch mixed with 2 tablespoons water (slurry)
- Cooked rice, for serving
- Optional: sliced green onions and sesame seeds for garnish

Instructions:

Marinating the Beef:

1. In a bowl, combine thinly sliced beef with soy sauce, oyster sauce, cornstarch, sesame oil, sugar, and black pepper. Mix well until the beef is evenly coated. Let it marinate for at least 30 minutes, or refrigerate for up to 2 hours.

Cooking the Stir-Fry:

1. Heat vegetable oil in a large skillet or wok over medium-high heat.
2. Add minced garlic and grated ginger to the skillet. Stir-fry for about 30 seconds until fragrant.

3. Add the marinated beef to the skillet in a single layer, allowing it to sear without overcrowding the pan. Cook for 1-2 minutes per side until browned. Remove the beef from the skillet and set aside.
4. In the same skillet, add broccoli florets and beef broth (or water). Cover and cook for about 3-4 minutes until the broccoli is tender-crisp.
5. Return the cooked beef to the skillet with the broccoli.
6. In a small bowl, mix together oyster sauce, soy sauce, hoisin sauce, and cornstarch slurry. Pour the sauce mixture over the beef and broccoli in the skillet.
7. Stir-fry for another 1-2 minutes until the sauce has thickened and coated the beef and broccoli evenly.
8. Remove from heat and transfer the Beef and Broccoli to a serving dish.
9. Serve hot over cooked rice, garnished with sliced green onions and sesame seeds if desired.

Enjoy your homemade Beef and Broccoli! Adjust the seasoning and thickness of the sauce according to your taste preference.

Lo Mein

Ingredients:

For the Sauce:

- 1/4 cup soy sauce
- 2 tablespoons oyster sauce
- 1 tablespoon hoisin sauce
- 1 tablespoon sesame oil
- 2 teaspoons sugar
- 1 teaspoon cornstarch
- 1/4 cup chicken broth or water

For the Lo Mein:

- 200g dried lo mein noodles or spaghetti
- 2 tablespoons vegetable oil, divided
- 2 boneless, skinless chicken breasts, thinly sliced
- Salt and pepper, to taste
- 2 cloves garlic, minced
- 1-inch piece of ginger, grated
- 1 onion, thinly sliced
- 1 bell pepper, thinly sliced
- 1 carrot, julienned
- 1 cup broccoli florets
- 1 cup sliced mushrooms
- 1 cup shredded cabbage
- Optional garnishes: sliced green onions, sesame seeds

Instructions:

Cooking the Noodles:

1. Cook the lo mein noodles according to the package instructions until al dente. Drain and rinse with cold water to stop the cooking process. Toss with 1 tablespoon of vegetable oil to prevent sticking. Set aside.

Making the Sauce:

1. In a small bowl, whisk together soy sauce, oyster sauce, hoisin sauce, sesame oil, sugar, cornstarch, and chicken broth (or water) until well combined. Set aside.

Cooking the Lo Mein:

1. Heat 1 tablespoon of vegetable oil in a large skillet or wok over medium-high heat.
2. Season the thinly sliced chicken breasts with salt and pepper. Add the chicken to the skillet and stir-fry for about 3-4 minutes until browned and cooked through. Remove the chicken from the skillet and set aside.
3. In the same skillet, add the remaining tablespoon of vegetable oil. Add minced garlic and grated ginger, and stir-fry for about 30 seconds until fragrant.
4. Add sliced onion, bell pepper, julienned carrot, broccoli florets, sliced mushrooms, and shredded cabbage to the skillet. Stir-fry for about 3-4 minutes until the vegetables are tender-crisp.
5. Return the cooked chicken to the skillet with the vegetables.
6. Pour the prepared sauce over the chicken and vegetables in the skillet. Stir well to coat everything evenly.
7. Add the cooked lo mein noodles to the skillet. Toss everything together until the noodles are heated through and evenly coated with the sauce.
8. Remove from heat and transfer the Chicken Lo Mein to a serving dish.
9. Garnish with sliced green onions and sesame seeds if desired.
10. Serve hot and enjoy your delicious homemade Chicken Lo Mein!

Feel free to customize this recipe by adding your favorite vegetables or protein such as shrimp, beef, or tofu. Adjust the seasoning and thickness of the sauce according to your taste preference.

Prawn Toast

Ingredients:

- 200g peeled and deveined prawns
- 2 slices white bread, crusts removed
- 1 egg white
- 1 tablespoon cornstarch
- 2 cloves garlic, minced
- 1 teaspoon grated ginger
- 1 tablespoon soy sauce
- 1 teaspoon sesame oil
- Salt and pepper, to taste
- Vegetable oil, for frying
- Sesame seeds, for garnish (optional)
- Sweet chili sauce or plum sauce, for dipping

Instructions:

1. In a food processor, combine the peeled and deveined prawns, garlic, ginger, soy sauce, sesame oil, egg white, and cornstarch. Season with salt and pepper. Blend until you have a smooth paste.
2. Spread the prawn mixture evenly onto the slices of bread.
3. Cut the bread into triangles or rectangles, depending on your preference.
4. Heat vegetable oil in a deep frying pan or wok over medium-high heat.
5. Once the oil is hot, carefully place the prawn toasts prawn-side down into the oil. Fry for about 2-3 minutes until golden brown and crispy.
6. Using tongs, carefully flip the prawn toasts and fry for an additional 1-2 minutes until the bread is golden brown and crispy.
7. Remove the prawn toasts from the oil and drain on paper towels to remove excess oil.
8. Sprinkle sesame seeds on top for garnish, if desired.
9. Serve the prawn toasts hot with sweet chili sauce or plum sauce for dipping.

Enjoy your homemade prawn toast as an appetizer or snack! Adjust the seasoning and spice level according to your taste preference.

Gong Bao Shrimp

Ingredients:

For the Marinade:

- 400g large shrimp, peeled and deveined
- 1 tablespoon soy sauce
- 1 tablespoon Shaoxing wine (or dry sherry)
- 1 teaspoon cornstarch

For the Sauce:

- 2 tablespoons soy sauce
- 1 tablespoon black vinegar (or rice vinegar)
- 1 tablespoon hoisin sauce
- 1 tablespoon oyster sauce
- 1 tablespoon sugar
- 1 teaspoon sesame oil

Other Ingredients:

- 2 tablespoons vegetable oil
- 3 cloves garlic, minced
- 1-inch piece of ginger, minced
- 1/2 cup unsalted peanuts
- 2-3 dried red chilies, chopped
- 3-4 green onions, chopped
- Cooked rice, for serving

Instructions:

1. In a bowl, combine the shrimp with soy sauce, Shaoxing wine, and cornstarch. Mix well and let it marinate for about 15-20 minutes.
2. In another bowl, mix together soy sauce, black vinegar, hoisin sauce, oyster sauce, sugar, and sesame oil to make the sauce. Set aside.
3. Heat vegetable oil in a wok or large skillet over medium-high heat. Add the minced garlic, ginger, chopped dried red chilies, and peanuts. Stir-fry for about 1-2 minutes until fragrant.
4. Add the marinated shrimp to the wok. Stir-fry for about 2-3 minutes until the shrimp turn pink and are cooked through.

5. Pour the sauce over the shrimp and peanuts. Stir well to coat the shrimp evenly with the sauce.
6. Add chopped green onions to the wok and stir-fry for another minute.
7. Remove from heat and transfer the Gong Bao Shrimp to a serving dish.
8. Serve hot with cooked rice.

Enjoy your delicious Gong Bao Shrimp! Adjust the amount of dried red chilies according to your spice preference.

Sweet Red Bean Paste Buns (Dou Sha Bao)

Ingredients:

For the Bun Dough:

- 2 cups all-purpose flour
- 2 teaspoons instant yeast
- 2 tablespoons sugar
- 1/2 teaspoon salt
- 3/4 cup warm milk
- 1 tablespoon vegetable oil

For the Sweet Red Bean Paste Filling:

- 1 cup cooked red beans (adzuki beans)
- 1/2 cup sugar
- 2 tablespoons vegetable oil
- 1/4 teaspoon salt
- 1 teaspoon vanilla extract (optional)

Instructions:

Making the Sweet Red Bean Paste Filling:

1. Rinse the cooked red beans under cold water and drain well.
2. In a saucepan, combine the cooked red beans, sugar, vegetable oil, and salt. Cook over medium heat, stirring constantly, until the mixture thickens and resembles a paste, about 10-15 minutes.
3. Remove from heat and stir in the vanilla extract if using. Let the sweet red bean paste cool completely before using as a filling for the buns.

Making the Bun Dough:

1. In a large bowl, combine the all-purpose flour, instant yeast, sugar, and salt. Mix well.
2. Gradually add the warm milk and vegetable oil to the dry ingredients, stirring until a dough forms.
3. Transfer the dough to a lightly floured surface and knead for about 5-7 minutes until smooth and elastic.
4. Place the dough in a greased bowl, cover with a clean kitchen towel, and let it rise in a warm place for about 1 hour or until doubled in size.

Assembling the Buns:

1. Punch down the risen dough and transfer it to a lightly floured surface. Divide the dough into equal-sized pieces, depending on how many buns you want to make.
2. Flatten each dough piece into a circle with your palm. Place a spoonful of sweet red bean paste filling in the center of each dough circle.
3. Gather the edges of the dough circle and pinch to seal, forming a bun with the filling enclosed inside.
4. Place the filled buns seam-side down on a parchment-lined baking sheet, leaving some space between each bun for them to rise.
5. Cover the buns with a clean kitchen towel and let them rise for another 30 minutes.

Baking the Buns:

1. Preheat the oven to 180°C (350°F).
2. Once the buns have risen, brush the tops with some milk or beaten egg for a shiny finish (optional).
3. Bake the buns in the preheated oven for about 15-20 minutes, or until golden brown.
4. Remove the buns from the oven and let them cool on a wire rack before serving.

Enjoy your homemade Sweet Red Bean Paste Buns (Dou Sha Bao)! Adjust the sweetness of the red bean paste filling according to your taste preference.

Shanghai-Style Lion's Head Meatballs

Ingredients:

For the Meatballs:

- 500g ground pork
- 1/2 cup breadcrumbs
- 1 egg
- 2 tablespoons soy sauce
- 1 tablespoon Shaoxing wine (or dry sherry)
- 2 teaspoons ginger, minced
- 2 cloves garlic, minced
- 1 teaspoon sugar
- 1/2 teaspoon salt
- 1/4 teaspoon white pepper
- 2 green onions, finely chopped
- 2 tablespoons vegetable oil (for frying)

For the Broth:

- 4 cups chicken broth
- 2 cups water
- 2 tablespoons soy sauce
- 1 tablespoon Shaoxing wine (or dry sherry)
- 1 tablespoon sugar
- 1 tablespoon sesame oil
- 2 cloves garlic, minced
- 1-inch piece ginger, sliced
- Salt and pepper, to taste

For Garnish:

- Bok choy or Napa cabbage leaves, blanched
- Sliced green onions
- Sesame seeds (optional)

Instructions:

Making the Meatballs:

1. In a large mixing bowl, combine ground pork, breadcrumbs, beaten egg, soy sauce, Shaoxing wine, minced ginger, minced garlic, sugar, salt, white pepper, and chopped green onions. Mix well until all ingredients are evenly distributed.
2. Shape the mixture into large meatballs, about 2-3 inches in diameter. Wetting your hands with water can help prevent sticking.
3. Heat vegetable oil in a large skillet over medium-high heat. Once hot, add the meatballs in batches, making sure not to overcrowd the pan. Fry until golden brown on all sides, about 3-4 minutes per side. Remove the meatballs from the skillet and set aside.

Making the Broth:

1. In a large pot, combine chicken broth, water, soy sauce, Shaoxing wine, sugar, sesame oil, minced garlic, sliced ginger, salt, and pepper. Bring the mixture to a simmer over medium heat.
2. Carefully add the fried meatballs to the simmering broth. Cover the pot and let the meatballs cook in the broth for about 20-25 minutes, or until cooked through and tender.

Serving:

1. Place blanched bok choy or Napa cabbage leaves in serving bowls.
2. Using a slotted spoon, transfer the cooked meatballs from the broth to the serving bowls.
3. Ladle the hot broth over the meatballs.
4. Garnish with sliced green onions and sesame seeds, if desired.
5. Serve hot with steamed rice.

Enjoy your homemade Shanghai-Style Lion's Head Meatballs! Adjust the seasoning of the broth to suit your taste preferences.

Cantonese Steamed Fish

Ingredients:

- 1 whole fish (such as sea bass, tilapia, or trout), cleaned and scaled
- 2-3 slices ginger
- 2 green onions, cut into long strips
- 2 tablespoons soy sauce
- 1 tablespoon oyster sauce
- 1 tablespoon Shaoxing wine (or dry sherry)
- 1 tablespoon sesame oil
- 1 teaspoon sugar
- 1/4 teaspoon white pepper
- 1 tablespoon vegetable oil
- Fresh cilantro (coriander) leaves, for garnish
- Sliced red chili (optional), for garnish

Instructions:

1. Rinse the whole fish under cold water, inside and out. Pat dry with paper towels.
2. Score the fish on both sides with 2-3 diagonal cuts, about 1 inch apart, to help it cook evenly and absorb flavors.
3. Place the fish on a heatproof plate that fits inside your steamer basket.
4. Place ginger slices and some of the green onion strips inside the cavity of the fish, and the remaining ginger and green onion on top.
5. In a small bowl, mix together soy sauce, oyster sauce, Shaoxing wine, sesame oil, sugar, and white pepper until well combined.
6. Pour the sauce evenly over the fish.
7. Fill a steamer pot with water and bring it to a boil over high heat. Once boiling, reduce the heat to medium.
8. Carefully place the plate with the fish into the steamer basket, making sure the water doesn't touch the bottom of the plate.
9. Cover the steamer pot with a lid and steam the fish for about 10-15 minutes, depending on the size and thickness of the fish, or until the flesh flakes easily with a fork and is opaque all the way through.
10. While the fish is steaming, heat vegetable oil in a small saucepan until shimmering. Remove from heat.
11. Once the fish is cooked, carefully remove the plate from the steamer basket and pour the hot oil over the fish. The oil will sizzle and help release the aromas of the ginger and green onion.

12. Garnish the fish with fresh cilantro leaves and sliced red chili, if using.
13. Serve the Cantonese Steamed Fish immediately with steamed rice and enjoy!

This dish is best served fresh and hot. Adjust the seasoning according to your taste preference.

Three Cup Chicken (San Bei Ji)

Ingredients:

- 500g chicken thighs or breast, cut into bite-sized pieces
- 1 tablespoon sesame oil
- 2 tablespoons soy sauce
- 2 tablespoons Shaoxing wine (or dry sherry)
- 2 tablespoons sugar
- 1-inch piece ginger, sliced
- 4 cloves garlic, minced
- 4-5 dried red chilies (optional)
- 1 cup fresh basil leaves
- 2 tablespoons vegetable oil
- Cooked rice, for serving

Instructions:

1. In a bowl, combine the chicken pieces with sesame oil, soy sauce, and Shaoxing wine. Mix well and let it marinate for about 15-30 minutes.
2. Heat vegetable oil in a wok or large skillet over medium-high heat. Add the sliced ginger and minced garlic, and sauté for about 1 minute until fragrant.
3. Add the marinated chicken pieces to the wok, along with the dried red chilies if using. Stir-fry the chicken for about 5-6 minutes until browned and cooked through.
4. Once the chicken is cooked, add the sugar to the wok and stir well to dissolve.
5. Add the fresh basil leaves to the wok and stir-fry for another minute until the basil leaves are wilted and aromatic.
6. Remove the Three Cup Chicken from the heat and transfer to a serving dish.
7. Serve hot with steamed rice.

Enjoy your homemade Three Cup Chicken! Adjust the amount of sugar and dried red chilies according to your taste preference.

Salt and Pepper Squid

Ingredients:

- 500g squid tubes, cleaned and sliced into rings
- 1 cup cornstarch
- 1 teaspoon salt
- 1 teaspoon black pepper
- 1 teaspoon five-spice powder (optional)
- Vegetable oil, for deep-frying
- 2 cloves garlic, minced
- 2 green onions, finely chopped
- 1 red chili, thinly sliced (optional)
- 1 tablespoon finely chopped cilantro (coriander), for garnish
- Lemon wedges, for serving

Instructions:

1. In a large bowl, combine cornstarch, salt, black pepper, and five-spice powder (if using). Mix well.
2. Heat vegetable oil in a deep fryer or large pot to 180°C (350°F).
3. Dredge the squid rings in the cornstarch mixture, shaking off any excess.
4. Carefully drop the coated squid rings into the hot oil in batches, making sure not to overcrowd the fryer. Fry for 2-3 minutes or until golden brown and crispy. Remove with a slotted spoon and drain on paper towels. Repeat with the remaining squid.
5. In a separate pan, heat a tablespoon of vegetable oil over medium heat. Add minced garlic and cook for about 30 seconds until fragrant.
6. Add the fried squid rings to the pan along with chopped green onions and sliced red chili (if using). Toss everything together for about a minute to heat through and coat the squid with the garlic and green onion.
7. Transfer the Salt and Pepper Squid to a serving plate, garnish with chopped cilantro, and serve immediately with lemon wedges on the side.
8. Enjoy your crispy and flavorful Salt and Pepper Squid as an appetizer or main dish!

Feel free to adjust the seasoning and spice level according to your taste preference. You can also serve the squid with a dipping sauce of your choice, such as sweet chili sauce or soy sauce mixed with lime juice and a pinch of sugar.

Chinese Hot Pot

Ingredients:

For the Broth:

- 6 cups chicken broth or vegetable broth
- 2 cups water
- 2 slices ginger
- 2 cloves garlic, crushed
- 2 green onions, chopped
- 2 tablespoons Shaoxing wine (or dry sherry)
- Salt and pepper, to taste

For the Hot Pot Ingredients (Choose a Variety):

- Thinly sliced meat (beef, lamb, pork, chicken)
- Seafood (shrimp, fish balls, squid, crab sticks)
- Tofu (firm tofu, tofu skin)
- Vegetables (Napa cabbage, spinach, bok choy, mushrooms, sliced potatoes)
- Noodles (udon, rice noodles, glass noodles)
- Dumplings (vegetarian, meat-filled)
- Eggs (quail eggs, tofu skin rolls)

For Dipping Sauces (Optional):

- Soy sauce
- Sesame oil
- Chili oil
- Chopped garlic
- Chopped scallions
- Chopped cilantro
- Hoisin sauce
- Peanut sauce

Instructions:

1. Prepare the Broth:
    1. In a large pot, combine chicken broth, water, ginger slices, crushed garlic, chopped green onions, and Shaoxing wine.

2. Bring the broth to a boil over high heat, then reduce the heat to low and let it simmer for about 20-30 minutes to allow the flavors to infuse. Season with salt and pepper to taste.

2. Set Up the Hot Pot:

   1. Place a portable electric or gas hot pot on the table and fill it with the prepared broth.
   2. Arrange the raw ingredients, such as thinly sliced meat, seafood, tofu, vegetables, noodles, and dumplings, on separate plates or platters around the hot pot.

3. Cooking in the Hot Pot:

   1. Once the broth is simmering, diners can use chopsticks or a ladle to add their desired ingredients to the hot pot.
   2. Allow the ingredients to cook in the broth until they are cooked through. Cooking times may vary depending on the ingredients, but typically meat and seafood cook quickly, while vegetables and dumplings may take longer.
   3. Retrieve cooked ingredients with chopsticks or a slotted spoon and transfer them to individual bowls.

4. Enjoy with Dipping Sauces (Optional):

   1. Set up a selection of dipping sauces on the table for diners to customize their flavors.
   2. Each person can create their own dipping sauce by combining soy sauce, sesame oil, chili oil, chopped garlic, chopped scallions, chopped cilantro, hoisin sauce, and/or peanut sauce in a small bowl.

5. Continue Cooking and Enjoying:

   1. As the meal progresses, continue adding more ingredients to the hot pot and enjoying the cooked food with dipping sauces.
   2. Adjust the heat of the hot pot as needed to maintain a gentle simmer.

6. Finish with Noodles:

   1. Towards the end of the meal, add noodles to the hot pot and cook until tender.
   2. Serve the noodles in individual bowls with some of the flavorful broth.

7. Enjoy the Experience:

   1. Chinese Hot Pot is a social and interactive dining experience, so take your time, enjoy the process of cooking and eating together, and savor the delicious flavors!

Feel free to customize your Chinese Hot Pot with your favorite ingredients and dipping sauces to suit your taste preferences. Enjoy!

Beef Chow Fun

Ingredients:

For the Marinade:

- 250g beef flank steak, thinly sliced against the grain
- 2 tablespoons soy sauce
- 1 tablespoon oyster sauce
- 1 teaspoon cornstarch
- 1 teaspoon sesame oil
- 1/2 teaspoon sugar
- 1/4 teaspoon black pepper

For the Sauce:

- 2 tablespoons soy sauce
- 1 tablespoon oyster sauce
- 1 tablespoon dark soy sauce (for color)
- 1 tablespoon Shaoxing wine (or dry sherry)
- 1 teaspoon sugar

Other Ingredients:

- 300g fresh wide rice noodles (chow fun noodles)
- 2 tablespoons vegetable oil
- 2 cloves garlic, minced
- 1-inch piece ginger, julienned
- 1 small onion, thinly sliced
- 1 bell pepper, thinly sliced
- 2 cups bean sprouts
- 2 green onions, cut into 2-inch lengths
- Salt and pepper, to taste
- Sesame oil, for drizzling (optional)
- Chopped cilantro (coriander) leaves, for garnish (optional)

Instructions:

1. Prepare the Beef:

1. In a bowl, combine thinly sliced beef with soy sauce, oyster sauce, cornstarch, sesame oil, sugar, and black pepper. Mix well and let it marinate for about 15-30 minutes.

2. Cook the Rice Noodles:
    1. If using fresh wide rice noodles, separate them gently to prevent sticking. If using dried rice noodles, soak them in hot water according to package instructions until softened, then drain well.
    2. Heat a large pot of water until boiling. Blanch the rice noodles in the boiling water for about 1-2 minutes until they are just cooked. Drain and rinse with cold water to stop the cooking process. Set aside.

3. Stir-Fry the Beef:
    1. Heat 1 tablespoon of vegetable oil in a wok or large skillet over high heat. Add the marinated beef slices and stir-fry for about 2-3 minutes until browned and cooked through. Remove the beef from the wok and set aside.

4. Stir-Fry the Vegetables:
    1. In the same wok or skillet, heat the remaining tablespoon of vegetable oil over high heat. Add minced garlic and julienned ginger, and stir-fry for about 30 seconds until fragrant.
    2. Add thinly sliced onion and bell pepper to the wok, and stir-fry for about 1-2 minutes until slightly softened.
    3. Add bean sprouts and green onions to the wok, and stir-fry for another minute until vegetables are crisp-tender.

5. Combine Everything:
    1. Return the cooked beef to the wok with the stir-fried vegetables.
    2. Add the cooked rice noodles to the wok.
    3. Pour the sauce mixture over the beef and noodles.
    4. Toss everything together until well combined and heated through. Season with salt and pepper to taste.

6. Serve:
    1. Transfer the Beef Chow Fun to a serving plate or dish.
    2. Drizzle with a little sesame oil for extra flavor, if desired.
    3. Garnish with chopped cilantro leaves, if using.
    4. Serve hot and enjoy your homemade Beef Chow Fun!

Feel free to customize this recipe by adding other vegetables or adjusting the seasoning to suit your taste preferences. Enjoy!

Ma La Xiang Guo (Spicy Numbing Stir-Fry)

Ingredients:

For the Sauce:

- 3 tablespoons soy sauce
- 2 tablespoons oyster sauce
- 2 tablespoons Chinese cooking wine (Shaoxing wine)
- 1 tablespoon sugar
- 1 tablespoon sesame oil
- 2 teaspoons cornstarch
- 1 teaspoon ground Sichuan peppercorns (or more to taste)
- 1 teaspoon chili flakes (or more to taste)

For the Stir-Fry:

- 300g mixed vegetables (such as bell peppers, mushrooms, broccoli, cauliflower, carrots, cabbage, baby corn, and snow peas), cut into bite-sized pieces
- 200g firm tofu, sliced into cubes
- 200g protein of your choice (such as chicken, beef, pork, shrimp, or a combination), thinly sliced
- 4 cloves garlic, minced
- 1-inch piece of ginger, minced
- 2-3 green onions, chopped
- 2 tablespoons vegetable oil
- Cooked rice or noodles, for serving

Instructions:

1. Prepare the Sauce:

    1. In a small bowl, whisk together soy sauce, oyster sauce, Chinese cooking wine, sugar, sesame oil, cornstarch, ground Sichuan peppercorns, and chili flakes until well combined. Set aside.

2. Prepare the Ingredients:

    1. Cut the mixed vegetables and protein of your choice into bite-sized pieces.
    2. Mince the garlic and ginger, and chop the green onions.

3. Stir-Fry the Ingredients:

1. Heat vegetable oil in a wok or large skillet over medium-high heat.
2. Add minced garlic and ginger to the wok, and stir-fry for about 30 seconds until fragrant.
3. Add the protein (such as chicken, beef, pork, or shrimp) to the wok, and stir-fry until cooked through.
4. Add the firm tofu cubes to the wok, and stir-fry for another minute until heated through.
5. Add the mixed vegetables to the wok, and stir-fry for 3-4 minutes until crisp-tender.

4. Add the Sauce:

   1. Give the sauce mixture a quick stir, then pour it over the stir-fried ingredients in the wok.
   2. Toss everything together until the sauce thickens and coats all the ingredients evenly.

5. Finish and Serve:

   1. Add chopped green onions to the wok, and toss everything together for another minute.
   2. Remove the Ma La Xiang Guo from the heat and transfer to a serving dish.
   3. Serve hot with cooked rice or noodles.

6. Enjoy:

   1. Serve Ma La Xiang Guo hot and enjoy the bold flavors and spicy kick!

Feel free to customize this recipe by adjusting the amount of Sichuan peppercorns and chili flakes to suit your spice preference. You can also add your favorite vegetables and protein to make it your own. Enjoy!

Scallion Pancakes

Ingredients:

- 2 cups all-purpose flour
- 1 cup hot water
- 1/2 teaspoon salt
- 2 tablespoons vegetable oil, plus more for frying
- 1 cup chopped scallions (green onions), both green and white parts
- Salt, to taste
- Sesame oil (optional), for brushing

Instructions:

1. Prepare the Dough:

    1. In a large mixing bowl, combine the all-purpose flour and salt.
    2. Gradually add the hot water to the flour mixture while stirring with chopsticks or a wooden spoon until a rough dough forms.
    3. Knead the dough in the bowl or on a lightly floured surface for about 5-7 minutes until smooth and elastic. If the dough is too dry, add a little more water, and if it's too sticky, add a little more flour.
    4. Cover the dough with a clean kitchen towel and let it rest for at least 30 minutes.

2. Roll Out the Pancakes:

    1. Divide the rested dough into 4 equal-sized portions.
    2. Roll out one portion of the dough on a lightly floured surface into a thin, flat circle, about 8 inches in diameter.
    3. Brush the surface of the rolled-out dough with vegetable oil.
    4. Sprinkle a generous amount of chopped scallions evenly over the oiled surface.
    5. Roll up the dough tightly into a long cylinder.
    6. Coil the cylinder into a spiral shape and then gently press it down to flatten it into a pancake shape, about 1/4 inch thick. Repeat with the remaining portions of dough.

3. Cook the Pancakes:

    1. Heat a thin layer of vegetable oil in a non-stick skillet or frying pan over medium heat.

2. Carefully transfer one scallion pancake to the hot skillet and cook for about 2-3 minutes on each side until golden brown and crispy, pressing down gently with a spatula to ensure even cooking.
3. Repeat with the remaining pancakes, adding more oil to the skillet as needed.

4. Serve:

   1. Once cooked, transfer the scallion pancakes to a cutting board and cut them into wedges or squares.
   2. Serve hot with dipping sauce or as a side dish.
   3. Optionally, brush the pancakes with a little sesame oil for extra flavor before serving.

5. Enjoy:

   1. Enjoy your homemade scallion pancakes while they're still warm and crispy!

Feel free to adjust the amount of scallions and salt according to your taste preferences. You can also experiment with adding other ingredients like sesame seeds or minced garlic to the dough for additional flavor.

Lion's Head Meatballs (Shi Zi Tou)

Ingredients:

For the Meatballs:

- 500g ground pork
- 1/2 cup breadcrumbs
- 1 egg
- 2 tablespoons soy sauce
- 2 teaspoons sesame oil
- 1 tablespoon Shaoxing wine (or dry sherry)
- 2 cloves garlic, minced
- 1 teaspoon grated ginger
- 1/2 teaspoon salt
- 1/4 teaspoon white pepper
- 2 green onions, finely chopped
- 2 tablespoons vegetable oil (for frying)

For the Broth:

- 4 cups chicken broth
- 2 cups water
- 2 tablespoons soy sauce
- 1 tablespoon Shaoxing wine (or dry sherry)
- 1 tablespoon sugar
- 1 tablespoon sesame oil
- 2 cloves garlic, minced
- 1-inch piece ginger, sliced
- Salt and pepper, to taste

For the Vegetables:

- 2 cups Napa cabbage, chopped
- 2 carrots, sliced
- 1 cup shiitake mushrooms, sliced
- 2 green onions, cut into 2-inch lengths

For Garnish:

- Chopped green onions
- Chopped cilantro (coriander) leaves

Instructions:

1. Prepare the Meatballs:
   1. In a large mixing bowl, combine ground pork, breadcrumbs, egg, soy sauce, sesame oil, Shaoxing wine, minced garlic, grated ginger, salt, white pepper, and chopped green onions. Mix well until thoroughly combined.
   2. Shape the mixture into large meatballs, about 2-3 inches in diameter.
   3. Heat vegetable oil in a large skillet over medium-high heat. Once hot, add the meatballs in batches and fry until golden brown on all sides, about 3-4 minutes per side. Transfer the browned meatballs to a plate and set aside.

2. Prepare the Broth:
   1. In a large pot, combine chicken broth, water, soy sauce, Shaoxing wine, sugar, sesame oil, minced garlic, sliced ginger, salt, and pepper. Bring the mixture to a boil over medium-high heat.
   2. Once boiling, reduce the heat to low and carefully add the browned meatballs to the broth.
   3. Cover and let the meatballs simmer in the broth for about 20-25 minutes, or until cooked through and tender.

3. Add the Vegetables:
   1. Add chopped Napa cabbage, sliced carrots, shiitake mushrooms, and green onions to the pot with the meatballs and broth.
   2. Simmer for an additional 10-15 minutes, or until the vegetables are tender.

4. Serve:
   1. Ladle the Lion's Head Meatballs and vegetables into serving bowls.
   2. Garnish with chopped green onions and cilantro leaves.
   3. Serve hot with steamed rice.

5. Enjoy:
   1. Enjoy your homemade Lion's Head Meatballs with the flavorful broth and tender vegetables!

Feel free to adjust the seasoning and add other vegetables according to your preference. Enjoy this comforting and hearty Chinese dish!

Fish Fragrant Eggplant (Yu Xiang Qie Zi)

Ingredients:

For the Eggplant:

- 2 large Chinese eggplants (or 1 large globe eggplant), cut into bite-sized pieces
- 1 teaspoon salt
- Vegetable oil, for frying

For the Sauce:

- 2 tablespoons soy sauce
- 1 tablespoon Chinkiang vinegar (or rice vinegar)
- 1 tablespoon sugar
- 1 tablespoon Shaoxing wine (or dry sherry)
- 1 tablespoon water
- 1 teaspoon cornstarch
- 2 teaspoons sesame oil

For Stir-Frying:

- 2 tablespoons vegetable oil
- 2 cloves garlic, minced
- 1-inch piece ginger, minced
- 2-3 green onions, chopped
- 2-3 dried red chilies, chopped (adjust to taste)
- 1/2 cup diced bell peppers (optional, for color)
- 1/2 cup diced carrots (optional, for color)
- 1/2 cup diced bamboo shoots (optional)
- 1/4 cup chopped cilantro (coriander) leaves, for garnish (optional)
- Cooked rice, for serving

Instructions:

1. Prepare the Eggplant:
    1. Place the chopped eggplant in a large bowl and sprinkle with salt. Toss to coat evenly and let it sit for about 15-20 minutes to draw out excess moisture.
    2. After 15-20 minutes, rinse the eggplant under cold water and pat dry with paper towels to remove excess salt and moisture.

2. Fry the Eggplant:
    1. Heat vegetable oil in a large skillet or wok over medium-high heat. Once hot, add the eggplant in batches and fry until golden brown and softened, about 3-4 minutes per batch. Remove the fried eggplant with a slotted spoon and transfer to a plate lined with paper towels to drain excess oil.

3. Make the Sauce:
    1. In a small bowl, mix together soy sauce, vinegar, sugar, Shaoxing wine, water, and cornstarch until well combined. Set aside.

4. Stir-Fry:
    1. Heat 2 tablespoons of vegetable oil in the same skillet or wok over medium heat. Add minced garlic, minced ginger, chopped green onions, and chopped dried red chilies. Stir-fry for about 1 minute until fragrant.
    2. If using, add diced bell peppers, carrots, and bamboo shoots to the skillet, and stir-fry for another 2-3 minutes until slightly softened.
    3. Return the fried eggplant to the skillet and pour the sauce over the eggplant and vegetables. Stir well to coat everything evenly.
    4. Cook for an additional 2-3 minutes until the sauce thickens slightly and coats the eggplant and vegetables.

5. Garnish and Serve:
    1. Remove the skillet from heat and transfer the Fish Fragrant Eggplant to a serving dish.
    2. Garnish with chopped cilantro leaves, if using.
    3. Serve hot with cooked rice.

6. Enjoy:
    1. Enjoy your homemade Fish Fragrant Eggplant with rice for a flavorful and satisfying meal!

Feel free to adjust the amount of dried red chilies to suit your spice preference. You can also add other vegetables or protein like tofu to make it a more substantial dish. Enjoy!

Szechuan Hot and Sour Soup

Ingredients:

- 4 cups chicken broth
- 2 cups water
- 100g firm tofu, diced into small cubes
- 50g wood ear mushrooms, rehydrated and thinly sliced
- 50g bamboo shoots, thinly sliced
- 2 eggs, beaten
- 2 tablespoons soy sauce
- 2 tablespoons Chinkiang vinegar (or rice vinegar)
- 1 tablespoon chili oil (adjust to taste)
- 1 tablespoon sesame oil
- 1 tablespoon cornstarch, dissolved in 2 tablespoons water
- 2 green onions, thinly sliced
- 2 cloves garlic, minced
- 1-inch piece ginger, grated
- Salt and white pepper, to taste
- Chopped cilantro (coriander), for garnish
- Sliced green onions, for garnish

Instructions:

1. Prepare Ingredients:

    1. Rehydrate wood ear mushrooms in warm water for about 15-20 minutes, then thinly slice them.
    2. In a small bowl, beat the eggs and set aside.
    3. Dissolve cornstarch in water and set aside.

2. Cook Soup Base:

    1. In a large pot, heat chicken broth and water over medium heat.
    2. Add diced tofu, sliced wood ear mushrooms, and sliced bamboo shoots to the pot.
    3. Stir in soy sauce, Chinkiang vinegar, chili oil, sesame oil, minced garlic, and grated ginger.
    4. Allow the soup to simmer for about 5 minutes to allow the flavors to meld.

3. Thicken Soup:

1. Once the soup is simmering, slowly pour in the beaten eggs in a steady stream while gently stirring the soup with a spoon or chopsticks.
2. Continue stirring for about 1 minute to create egg ribbons in the soup.
3. Stir the cornstarch mixture to recombine and then pour it into the soup while stirring constantly.
4. Cook for an additional 1-2 minutes until the soup thickens slightly.

4. Season and Garnish:

1. Season the soup with salt and white pepper to taste.
2. Stir in sliced green onions.
3. Ladle the Szechuan Hot and Sour Soup into serving bowls.
4. Garnish with chopped cilantro and additional sliced green onions if desired.

5. Serve:

1. Serve the Szechuan Hot and Sour Soup hot as an appetizer or as part of a Chinese meal.
2. Enjoy the bold flavors and spicy kick of this delicious homemade soup!

Feel free to adjust the amount of chili oil according to your spice preference. You can also add other ingredients like shredded chicken, shiitake mushrooms, or baby corn for extra flavor and texture. Enjoy!

Shrimp Dumplings (Har Gow)

Ingredients:

For the Dumpling Filling:

- 250g raw shrimp, peeled, deveined, and finely chopped
- 1 tablespoon cornstarch
- 1 tablespoon soy sauce
- 1 teaspoon sesame oil
- 1 teaspoon sugar
- 1/2 teaspoon salt
- 1/4 teaspoon white pepper
- 1/2 teaspoon grated ginger
- 1/2 cup bamboo shoots, finely chopped (optional)
- 2 green onions, finely chopped

For the Dumpling Wrapper:

- 1 cup wheat starch
- 1/4 cup tapioca starch
- 1/4 teaspoon salt
- 1 cup boiling water
- 1 teaspoon vegetable oil

For Garnish (Optional):

- Toasted sesame seeds
- Sliced green onions

Instructions:

1. Prepare the Dumpling Filling:
    1. In a bowl, combine chopped shrimp, cornstarch, soy sauce, sesame oil, sugar, salt, white pepper, grated ginger, chopped bamboo shoots (if using), and chopped green onions. Mix well until everything is evenly combined. Set aside.

2. Make the Dumpling Wrapper Dough:
    1. In a large mixing bowl, combine wheat starch, tapioca starch, and salt.
    2. Gradually add boiling water to the dry ingredients while stirring continuously with a spoon or chopsticks until a dough forms.

3. Knead the dough with your hands until smooth and elastic. If the dough is too dry, add a little more boiling water; if it's too wet, add a little more wheat starch.
4. Divide the dough into small balls, about 1 tablespoon each, and keep them covered with a damp cloth to prevent drying out.

3. Roll out the Dumpling Wrappers:

   1. Take one dough ball and roll it out into a thin, round wrapper, about 3 inches in diameter, using a rolling pin on a lightly floured surface.
   2. Repeat with the remaining dough balls, keeping the wrappers covered with a damp cloth to prevent them from drying out.

4. Fill and Shape the Dumplings:

   1. Place a spoonful of the shrimp filling in the center of each wrapper.
   2. Fold the wrapper in half to enclose the filling, forming a half-moon shape.
   3. Use your fingers to pleat and seal the edges of the wrapper, creating a crimped pattern along the top edge.
   4. Repeat with the remaining wrappers and filling.

5. Steam the Dumplings:

   1. Arrange the shrimp dumplings on a lightly greased steamer basket, making sure they're not touching each other.
   2. Steam the dumplings over boiling water for about 8-10 minutes, or until the wrappers are translucent and the shrimp filling is cooked through.

6. Garnish and Serve:

   1. Remove the steamed shrimp dumplings from the steamer and transfer them to a serving plate.
   2. Garnish with toasted sesame seeds and sliced green onions, if desired.
   3. Serve hot with soy sauce, chili oil, or your favorite dipping sauce.

7. Enjoy:

   1. Enjoy your homemade shrimp dumplings (Har Gow) as a delicious appetizer or part of a dim sum feast!

Feel free to adjust the filling ingredients and seasonings according to your taste preferences. These dumplings are best enjoyed fresh and hot, but you can also freeze them before steaming for later use. Enjoy!

Steamed Buns (Baozi)

Ingredients:

For the Dough:

- 3 cups all-purpose flour
- 2 teaspoons instant yeast
- 3 tablespoons sugar
- 1 teaspoon salt
- 1 cup warm water
- 1 tablespoon vegetable oil

For the Filling (Choose one or more):

- BBQ pork (Char Siu)
- Ground pork with vegetables
- Red bean paste
- Custard

For Cooking:

- Vegetable oil or parchment paper, for lining the steamer

Instructions:

1. Prepare the Dough:

1. In a large mixing bowl, combine all-purpose flour, instant yeast, sugar, and salt.
2. Gradually add warm water to the dry ingredients while stirring with a spoon or spatula.
3. Once the dough starts to come together, knead it with your hands until smooth and elastic, about 8-10 minutes.
4. Shape the dough into a ball and place it back in the mixing bowl. Cover with a clean kitchen towel and let it rest in a warm, draft-free place for about 1 hour, or until it doubles in size.

2. Prepare the Filling:

1. While the dough is resting, prepare your desired filling. For savory buns, you can use BBQ pork (Char Siu), ground pork with vegetables, or any other savory filling of your choice. For sweet buns, you can use red bean paste or custard.

3. Shape the Buns:
    1. After the dough has doubled in size, punch it down to release any air bubbles.
    2. Transfer the dough to a lightly floured surface and divide it into equal-sized portions, depending on how large you want your buns to be.
    3. Flatten each portion of dough into a small circle with your hands or a rolling pin.
    4. Place a spoonful of filling in the center of each dough circle.
    5. Gather the edges of the dough circle and pinch them together at the top to seal the bun, forming a pleated pattern if desired. Repeat with the remaining dough and filling.

4. Steam the Buns:
    1. Line a steamer basket with vegetable oil or parchment paper to prevent the buns from sticking.
    2. Place the filled buns in the steamer basket, leaving some space between them to expand.
    3. Cover the steamer basket with a lid and let the buns rest for about 15-20 minutes to rise slightly.
    4. Meanwhile, bring water to a boil in the steamer.
    5. Once the water is boiling, place the steamer basket over the boiling water and steam the buns for about 12-15 minutes, or until they are puffed up and cooked through.

5. Serve:
    1. Remove the steamed buns from the steamer and transfer them to a serving plate.
    2. Serve the steamed buns hot as a snack, appetizer, or part of a meal.
    3. Enjoy your homemade steamed buns with your favorite dipping sauce or condiments.

6. Enjoy:
    1. Enjoy your homemade steamed buns (Baozi) filled with delicious savory or sweet fillings!

Feel free to customize the filling according to your preferences and experiment with different flavors and ingredients. These steamed buns are best enjoyed fresh and hot, but you can also store any leftovers in an airtight container in the refrigerator and reheat them before serving. Enjoy!

Stir-Fried Snow Peas with Garlic

Ingredients:

- 250g snow peas, ends trimmed
- 2 tablespoons vegetable oil
- 3 cloves garlic, thinly sliced
- 1 tablespoon soy sauce
- 1 teaspoon sesame oil
- Salt and pepper, to taste
- Sesame seeds, for garnish (optional)
- Sliced green onions, for garnish (optional)

Instructions:

1. Prepare the Snow Peas:

1. Rinse the snow peas under cold water and pat them dry with a kitchen towel.
2. Trim the ends of the snow peas if necessary.

2. Heat the Wok or Skillet:

1. Heat vegetable oil in a wok or large skillet over medium-high heat until hot but not smoking.

3. Stir-Fry Snow Peas:

1. Add sliced garlic to the hot oil and stir-fry for about 30 seconds to 1 minute until fragrant, being careful not to burn the garlic.
2. Add the snow peas to the wok or skillet and stir-fry for 2-3 minutes, tossing frequently, until they are bright green and slightly tender but still crisp.
3. Season the snow peas with soy sauce, sesame oil, salt, and pepper. Continue to stir-fry for another 1-2 minutes until the snow peas are evenly coated with the seasonings and heated through.

4. Garnish and Serve:

1. Transfer the stir-fried snow peas to a serving dish.
2. Garnish with sesame seeds and sliced green onions, if desired, for extra flavor and presentation.

5. Enjoy:

1. Serve the stir-fried snow peas with garlic hot as a side dish or as part of a larger meal.
2. Enjoy the delicious crunch and vibrant flavors of this simple yet satisfying dish!

Feel free to adjust the seasoning and add other ingredients like sliced bell peppers, mushrooms, or carrots for added color and flavor. Serve the stir-fried snow peas with steamed rice or noodles for a complete meal. Enjoy!

Crispy Duck Pancakes

Ingredients:

For the Duck:

- 1 whole duck (about 2-3 kg)
- 2 tablespoons Chinese five-spice powder
- 2 tablespoons honey
- 2 tablespoons soy sauce
- 1 tablespoon rice vinegar
- Salt, to taste

For Serving:

- Thin Chinese pancakes (store-bought or homemade)
- Hoisin sauce
- 1 cucumber, julienned
- 2-3 green onions, thinly sliced

Instructions:

1. Prepare the Duck:

    1. Preheat your oven to 180°C (350°F).
    2. Rinse the duck inside and out under cold water, then pat dry with paper towels.
    3. In a small bowl, mix together Chinese five-spice powder, honey, soy sauce, rice vinegar, and a pinch of salt to create a marinade.
    4. Brush the marinade all over the duck, both inside and out, ensuring it is evenly coated.
    5. Place the duck on a wire rack set over a baking tray, breast side up.
    6. Roast the duck in the preheated oven for 1.5 to 2 hours, or until the skin is crispy and golden brown and the internal temperature reaches 75°C (165°F).
    7. Once cooked, remove the duck from the oven and let it rest for 10-15 minutes before carving.

2. Carve the Duck:

    1. Carefully carve the crispy skin and tender meat from the duck, slicing it into thin strips.
    2. Arrange the sliced duck meat on a serving platter.

3. Assemble the Pancakes:
    1. Heat the Chinese pancakes according to the package instructions, or lightly steam them to make them soft and pliable.
    2. To assemble each pancake, spread a thin layer of hoisin sauce on one side of the pancake.
    3. Place a few slices of cucumber and green onion on top of the hoisin sauce.
    4. Add a few slices of the crispy duck on top of the vegetables.

4. Roll Up and Serve:
    1. Roll up the pancake tightly to enclose the filling, similar to a burrito.
    2. Repeat with the remaining pancakes and filling.
    3. Serve the crispy duck pancakes immediately, either as an appetizer or as part of a larger meal.

5. Enjoy:
    1. Enjoy your homemade crispy duck pancakes with their delicious combination of flavors and textures!

Feel free to adjust the filling ingredients according to your preference. You can also add other condiments such as sliced spring onions, shredded lettuce, or even sliced chili for added flavor and heat.

Taiwanese Beef Noodle Soup

Ingredients:

For the Beef Broth:

- 2 lbs beef bones (such as marrow or knuckle bones)
- 1 lb beef shank or brisket, cut into chunks
- 1 onion, peeled and halved
- 4 cloves garlic, smashed
- 2-inch piece of ginger, sliced
- 2 cinnamon sticks
- 4 star anise
- 4 dried bay leaves
- 1 tablespoon Sichuan peppercorns
- 1/4 cup soy sauce
- 2 tablespoons dark soy sauce
- 2 tablespoons Shaoxing wine (or dry sherry)
- 2 tablespoons rock sugar (or granulated sugar)
- Salt, to taste
- Water, as needed

For the Soup:

- 1 lb fresh or dried Chinese wheat noodles
- 1 lb beef chuck or flank steak, thinly sliced
- 2 cups baby bok choy or Shanghai bok choy, chopped
- 4 green onions, chopped
- 1/4 cup cilantro (coriander) leaves, chopped
- Chili oil, for serving (optional)

Instructions:

1. Prepare the Beef Broth:

    1. Rinse the beef bones under cold water and place them in a large stockpot.
    2. Add the beef shank or brisket chunks, onion halves, smashed garlic cloves, sliced ginger, cinnamon sticks, star anise, bay leaves, and Sichuan peppercorns to the pot.
    3. Pour in enough water to cover all the ingredients in the pot.
    4. Add soy sauce, dark soy sauce, Shaoxing wine, and rock sugar to the pot.

5. Bring the broth to a boil over high heat, then reduce the heat to low and simmer, uncovered, for 2-3 hours, skimming off any impurities and foam that rise to the surface.
6. Once the broth is rich and flavorful, strain it through a fine-mesh sieve into a clean pot or container. Discard the solids. Season the broth with salt to taste.

2. Cook the Noodles and Beef:

1. Cook the Chinese wheat noodles according to the package instructions until al dente. Drain and set aside.
2. Bring the beef broth back to a simmer over medium heat.
3. Add the thinly sliced beef chuck or flank steak to the simmering broth and cook for 1-2 minutes until the beef is just cooked through.
4. Use a slotted spoon to remove the cooked beef from the broth and set it aside.

3. Assemble the Soup:

1. Divide the cooked noodles among serving bowls.
2. Top the noodles with the cooked beef slices, chopped baby bok choy, green onions, and cilantro leaves.
3. Ladle the hot beef broth over the noodles and beef, ensuring each bowl is generously filled with broth.
4. Serve the Taiwanese Beef Noodle Soup hot, with chili oil on the side for those who enjoy extra heat.

4. Enjoy:

1. Enjoy your homemade Taiwanese Beef Noodle Soup, savoring the rich broth, tender beef, and chewy noodles!

Feel free to customize the soup by adding other toppings such as blanched bean sprouts, pickled mustard greens, or sliced radishes. Adjust the seasoning and spice level according to your taste preference. This comforting and flavorful soup is perfect for a cozy meal on a chilly day.

Chinese BBQ Ribs

Ingredients:

For the Marinade:

- 1 rack of pork spare ribs or baby back ribs (about 2-3 lbs)
- 3 cloves garlic, minced
- 2 tablespoons hoisin sauce
- 2 tablespoons soy sauce
- 2 tablespoons honey
- 1 tablespoon Chinese rice wine (or dry sherry)
- 1 tablespoon sesame oil
- 1 tablespoon Chinese five-spice powder
- 1 teaspoon ground white pepper
- 1 teaspoon red food coloring (optional, for traditional red color)
- Salt, to taste

For the Glaze:

- 2 tablespoons honey
- 1 tablespoon hoisin sauce
- 1 tablespoon soy sauce
- 1 tablespoon Chinese rice wine (or dry sherry)
- 1 teaspoon sesame oil

For Garnish:

- Toasted sesame seeds
- Thinly sliced green onions

Instructions:

1. Prepare the Ribs:
    1. Rinse the rack of ribs under cold water and pat them dry with paper towels.
    2. If using spare ribs, remove the tough membrane from the back of the ribs.
    3. Place the ribs in a shallow dish or a large resealable plastic bag.

2. Make the Marinade:

1. In a bowl, mix together minced garlic, hoisin sauce, soy sauce, honey, Chinese rice wine, sesame oil, Chinese five-spice powder, ground white pepper, and red food coloring (if using).
2. Pour the marinade over the ribs, making sure they are evenly coated on all sides. Cover the dish or seal the bag and refrigerate for at least 4 hours, or preferably overnight, to marinate.

3. Preheat the Oven:

    1. Preheat your oven to 180°C (350°F).

4. Bake the Ribs:

    1. Remove the marinated ribs from the refrigerator and let them come to room temperature while the oven preheats.
    2. Line a baking sheet with aluminum foil for easy cleanup.
    3. Place the ribs on the prepared baking sheet, meaty side up.
    4. Bake the ribs in the preheated oven for 45-60 minutes, or until they are tender and cooked through. You can also baste the ribs with the marinade halfway through baking for extra flavor.

5. Make the Glaze:

    1. In a small saucepan, combine honey, hoisin sauce, soy sauce, Chinese rice wine, and sesame oil.
    2. Heat the glaze over medium heat, stirring constantly, until it thickens slightly, about 2-3 minutes. Remove from heat.

6. Glaze the Ribs:

    1. Once the ribs are cooked, remove them from the oven and brush them generously with the prepared glaze.
    2. Return the glazed ribs to the oven and broil them for 2-3 minutes, or until the glaze is caramelized and sticky. Keep a close eye on them to prevent burning.

7. Serve:

    1. Remove the Chinese BBQ ribs from the oven and let them rest for a few minutes.
    2. Slice the ribs between the bones into individual portions.
    3. Garnish with toasted sesame seeds and thinly sliced green onions, if desired.
    4. Serve the Chinese BBQ ribs hot as a delicious appetizer or main dish.

8. Enjoy:

1. Enjoy your homemade Chinese BBQ ribs, savoring their sweet, savory, and sticky goodness!

Feel free to adjust the marinade ingredients according to your taste preferences. You can also grill the ribs instead of baking them for a smokier flavor. Serve the ribs with steamed rice and stir-fried vegetables for a complete meal.

Eight Treasure Rice (Ba Bao Fan)

Ingredients:

For the Glutinous Rice:

- 2 cups glutinous rice (also known as sticky rice)
- 2 cups water

For the Toppings:

- 1/2 cup red bean paste
- 1/2 cup cooked black glutinous rice (also known as black sticky rice)
- 1/2 cup cooked sweetened lotus seeds
- 1/2 cup cooked sweetened dried fruits (such as apricots, dates, or raisins)
- 1/2 cup cooked sweetened chestnuts
- 1/2 cup cooked sweetened mung beans
- 1/2 cup cooked sweetened red beans
- 1/2 cup cooked sweetened peanuts
- 1/2 cup cooked sweetened lotus seeds
- 1/4 cup honey or syrup, for drizzling (optional)

For Garnish (Optional):

- Toasted sesame seeds
- Sliced almonds
- Dried fruit slices

Instructions:

1. Prepare the Glutinous Rice:

   1. Rinse the glutinous rice under cold water until the water runs clear.
   2. Place the rinsed rice in a bowl and cover it with water. Let it soak for at least 4 hours or overnight.

2. Cook the Glutinous Rice:

   1. Drain the soaked rice and place it in a steamer basket lined with cheesecloth or a clean kitchen towel.
   2. Steam the rice over boiling water for about 25-30 minutes, or until it is tender and cooked through.

3. Assemble the Eight Treasure Rice:
    1. Once the glutinous rice is cooked, transfer it to a large mixing bowl.
    2. Divide the cooked rice into 8 equal portions.
    3. Arrange one portion of the cooked glutinous rice in the center of a serving plate.
    4. Arrange the cooked sweetened toppings (red bean paste, black glutinous rice, sweetened lotus seeds, dried fruits, chestnuts, mung beans, red beans, and peanuts) around the rice, creating a colorful pattern.
    5. Repeat with the remaining portions of cooked rice and toppings, layering them on top of each other to create a mound or dome shape.
    6. Drizzle honey or syrup over the top of the Eight Treasure Rice, if desired.

4. Garnish and Serve:
    1. Garnish the Eight Treasure Rice with toasted sesame seeds, sliced almonds, and dried fruit slices, if desired.
    2. Serve the Eight Treasure Rice warm or at room temperature as a delicious and visually stunning dessert.

5. Enjoy:
    1. Enjoy your homemade Eight Treasure Rice, savoring the combination of sweet and savory flavors and the chewy texture of the glutinous rice and toppings!

Feel free to customize the toppings according to your taste preferences and the availability of ingredients. You can also adjust the sweetness of the toppings by adding more or less sugar or honey during the cooking process. Serve the Eight Treasure Rice as a festive dessert for special occasions or as a comforting treat any time of the year.

Braised Pork Belly (Hong Shao Rou)

Ingredients:

For the Pork Belly:

- 1 lb pork belly, skin-on
- 2 tablespoons vegetable oil
- 2 slices ginger
- 2 green onions, cut into sections
- 2 cloves garlic, smashed

For the Braising Sauce:

- 2 tablespoons soy sauce
- 2 tablespoons dark soy sauce
- 2 tablespoons Shaoxing wine (or dry sherry)
- 2 tablespoons rock sugar (or granulated sugar)
- 1 star anise
- 2 dried bay leaves
- 1 cinnamon stick
- 1 cup water or chicken broth

For Garnish (Optional):

- Sliced green onions
- Toasted sesame seeds

Instructions:

1. Prepare the Pork Belly:
    1. Rinse the pork belly under cold water and pat it dry with paper towels.
    2. Cut the pork belly into bite-sized pieces, about 1-inch cubes.

2. Brown the Pork Belly:
    1. Heat vegetable oil in a large skillet or wok over medium heat.
    2. Add the pork belly pieces to the hot oil and cook until they are golden brown on all sides, about 5-7 minutes.
    3. Remove the browned pork belly from the skillet and set it aside.

3. Make the Braising Sauce:

1. In the same skillet or wok, add ginger slices, green onion sections, and smashed garlic cloves. Stir-fry for 1-2 minutes until fragrant.
2. Add soy sauce, dark soy sauce, Shaoxing wine, rock sugar, star anise, dried bay leaves, and cinnamon stick to the skillet. Stir to combine.
3. Return the browned pork belly to the skillet, coating it with the sauce mixture.

4. Braise the Pork Belly:

   1. Pour water or chicken broth into the skillet until the pork belly is almost covered with liquid.
   2. Bring the sauce to a simmer over medium heat, then reduce the heat to low.
   3. Cover the skillet with a lid and let the pork belly braise for 1.5 to 2 hours, stirring occasionally, until the meat is tender and the sauce has thickened.
   4. If the sauce thickens too quickly or the pork belly is not yet tender, add more water or broth as needed and continue to simmer.

5. Serve:

   1. Once the pork belly is tender and the sauce has thickened to your liking, remove the skillet from the heat.
   2. Transfer the braised pork belly to a serving dish and garnish with sliced green onions and toasted sesame seeds, if desired.
   3. Serve the braised pork belly hot as a delicious main dish, accompanied by steamed rice or vegetables.

6. Enjoy:

   1. Enjoy your homemade braised pork belly (Hong Shao Rou), savoring its rich and savory flavor and melt-in-your-mouth texture!

Feel free to adjust the seasoning and spice level according to your taste preferences.

You can also add other aromatics such as star anise, cloves, or ginger for extra flavor.

Serve the braised pork belly with steamed buns or noodles for a comforting and satisfying meal.

Stir-Fried Green Beans with Minced Pork

Ingredients:

For the Stir-Fry:

- 1 lb green beans, trimmed and cut into bite-sized pieces
- 1/2 lb ground pork
- 2 tablespoons vegetable oil
- 3 cloves garlic, minced
- 1-inch piece of ginger, minced
- 2 green onions, chopped
- Salt and pepper, to taste

For the Sauce:

- 2 tablespoons soy sauce
- 1 tablespoon oyster sauce
- 1 tablespoon Shaoxing wine (or dry sherry)
- 1 teaspoon sesame oil
- 1 teaspoon sugar
- 1 teaspoon cornstarch
- 2 tablespoons water

Optional Garnish:

- Toasted sesame seeds
- Sliced green onions

Instructions:

1. Blanch the Green Beans:

   1. Bring a pot of water to a boil. Add the green beans and blanch for 2-3 minutes, or until they are bright green and crisp-tender.
   2. Drain the green beans and rinse them under cold water to stop the cooking process. Set aside.

2. Prepare the Sauce:

   1. In a small bowl, whisk together soy sauce, oyster sauce, Shaoxing wine, sesame oil, sugar, cornstarch, and water until well combined. Set aside.

3. Stir-Fry the Pork:
    1. Heat vegetable oil in a large skillet or wok over medium-high heat.
    2. Add minced garlic and ginger to the hot oil and stir-fry for about 30 seconds, or until fragrant.
    3. Add the ground pork to the skillet, breaking it up with a spatula, and cook until it is browned and cooked through.
    4. Stir in chopped green onions and cook for another minute.

4. Add the Green Beans:
    1. Add the blanched green beans to the skillet with the cooked pork mixture.
    2. Stir-fry the green beans and pork together for 2-3 minutes, or until the beans are heated through and well-coated with the pork mixture.

5. Add the Sauce:
    1. Give the sauce mixture a quick stir to recombine, then pour it over the green beans and pork in the skillet.
    2. Stir-fry everything together for another 1-2 minutes, or until the sauce has thickened slightly and evenly coats the green beans and pork.

6. Garnish and Serve:
    1. Transfer the stir-fried green beans with minced pork to a serving dish.
    2. Garnish with toasted sesame seeds and sliced green onions, if desired.
    3. Serve hot as a delicious main dish, accompanied by steamed rice.

7. Enjoy:
    1. Enjoy your homemade stir-fried green beans with minced pork, savoring the combination of tender green beans and flavorful pork!

Feel free to adjust the seasoning and add other vegetables such as bell peppers or carrots to the stir-fry for added color and flavor. You can also add a sprinkle of red pepper flakes for a spicy kick if desired.

Clay Pot Rice (Bao Zai Fan)

Ingredients:

For the Rice and Meat:

- 2 cups jasmine rice, rinsed and drained
- 1 lb boneless chicken thighs, diced (or your choice of protein such as pork, beef, or seafood)
- 2 Chinese sausages (lap cheong), sliced
- 2 cups chicken broth (or water)
- 2 tablespoons vegetable oil
- 2 cloves garlic, minced
- 1 tablespoon ginger, minced
- Salt and pepper, to taste

For the Sauce:

- 2 tablespoons soy sauce
- 2 tablespoons oyster sauce
- 1 tablespoon dark soy sauce
- 1 tablespoon Shaoxing wine (or dry sherry)
- 1 teaspoon sesame oil
- 1 teaspoon sugar

Optional Garnish:

- Sliced green onions
- Toasted sesame seeds
- Sliced red chili

Instructions:

1. Prepare the Sauce:

    1. In a small bowl, whisk together soy sauce, oyster sauce, dark soy sauce, Shaoxing wine, sesame oil, and sugar until well combined. Set aside.

2. Marinate the Meat:

    1. Place the diced chicken thighs (or other protein) in a bowl and season with salt and pepper.

2. Add half of the prepared sauce to the bowl and toss to coat the meat evenly. Set aside to marinate for at least 15-20 minutes.

3. Rinse and Soak the Rice:

    1. Rinse the jasmine rice under cold water until the water runs clear.
    2. Place the rinsed rice in a bowl and cover it with water. Let it soak for at least 20-30 minutes, then drain.

4. Cook the Rice and Meat:

    1. Heat vegetable oil in a clay pot or large skillet over medium heat.
    2. Add minced garlic and ginger to the hot oil and stir-fry for about 1-2 minutes until fragrant.
    3. Add the marinated chicken thighs and Chinese sausages to the pot and cook until they are browned and cooked through, about 5-7 minutes.
    4. Remove the cooked meat from the pot and set it aside.

5. Cook the Rice:

    1. In the same pot, add the soaked and drained rice.
    2. Pour chicken broth (or water) over the rice, making sure the liquid covers the rice by about 1/2 inch.
    3. Bring the liquid to a boil over high heat, then reduce the heat to low and cover the pot with a lid.
    4. Let the rice simmer for about 15-20 minutes, or until the liquid is absorbed and the rice is cooked through.

6. Combine Rice and Meat:

    1. Once the rice is cooked, add the cooked chicken thighs and Chinese sausages back to the pot.
    2. Pour the remaining sauce over the rice and meat mixture.
    3. Gently stir everything together to combine.

7. Finish and Serve:

    1. Continue to cook the rice and meat mixture for another 2-3 minutes, stirring occasionally, until the sauce is heated through and evenly coats the rice and meat.
    2. Garnish with sliced green onions, toasted sesame seeds, and sliced red chili, if desired.
    3. Serve the clay pot rice hot as a delicious and comforting meal.

8. Enjoy:

    1. Enjoy your homemade clay pot rice (Bao Zai Fan), savoring the aromatic flavors and hearty texture of this classic Cantonese dish!

Feel free to customize the dish by adding other ingredients such as mushrooms, Chinese vegetables, or seafood to the rice and meat mixture. Adjust the seasoning and sauce according to your taste preferences. The clay pot gives the rice a crispy layer on the bottom, known as "guo ba," which adds an extra layer of texture and flavor to the dish.

Zhajiangmian (Noodles with Soybean Paste)

Ingredients:

For the Noodles:

- 12 oz fresh or dried noodles (such as wheat noodles or egg noodles)

For the Zhajiang Sauce:

- 2 tablespoons vegetable oil
- 1/2 lb ground pork (or beef)
- 3 cloves garlic, minced
- 2 tablespoons fermented soybean paste (zhajiang)
- 1 tablespoon hoisin sauce
- 1 tablespoon soy sauce
- 1 teaspoon sugar
- 1/2 cup water
- Salt and pepper, to taste

For Serving:

- Thinly sliced cucumbers
- Julienned carrots
- Thinly sliced green onions
- Chopped cilantro (optional)
- Chili oil (optional)
- Toasted sesame seeds (optional)

Instructions:

1. Cook the Noodles:
    1. Bring a large pot of water to a boil. Cook the noodles according to the package instructions until they are al dente. If using fresh noodles, this will only take a few minutes. If using dried noodles, it may take a little longer.
    2. Once cooked, drain the noodles and rinse them under cold water to stop the cooking process. Set aside.

2. Prepare the Zhajiang Sauce:
    1. Heat vegetable oil in a large skillet or wok over medium-high heat.
    2. Add minced garlic to the hot oil and stir-fry for about 30 seconds until fragrant.

3. Add the ground pork (or beef) to the skillet and cook until it is browned and cooked through.
4. Add fermented soybean paste (zhajiang), hoisin sauce, soy sauce, and sugar to the skillet, stirring to combine.
5. Pour water into the skillet and stir well to incorporate the ingredients.
6. Reduce the heat to low and let the sauce simmer for about 5-7 minutes, allowing it to thicken slightly.
7. Season the sauce with salt and pepper to taste.

3. Assemble and Serve:

1. Divide the cooked noodles among serving bowls.
2. Ladle the zhajiang sauce over the noodles, ensuring each bowl gets a generous amount of sauce.
3. Top the noodles and sauce with thinly sliced cucumbers, julienned carrots, thinly sliced green onions, and chopped cilantro, if using.
4. Drizzle chili oil over the top for extra heat, if desired.
5. Sprinkle toasted sesame seeds over the dish for added flavor and texture.
6. Serve the Zhajiangmian immediately, allowing diners to mix the noodles and sauce together before eating.

4. Enjoy:

1. Enjoy your homemade Zhajiangmian, savoring the rich and savory flavors of the fermented soybean paste sauce paired with the noodles and fresh vegetables!

Feel free to customize the dish by adding other toppings such as shredded lettuce, bean sprouts, or sliced radishes. Adjust the amount of chili oil according to your spice preference. Serve the Zhajiangmian as a delicious and satisfying meal for lunch or dinner.

Crispy Shredded Beef

Ingredients:

For the Marinated Beef:

- 1 lb beef sirloin or flank steak, thinly sliced against the grain
- 2 tablespoons soy sauce
- 1 tablespoon Shaoxing wine (or dry sherry)
- 1 teaspoon sesame oil
- 1 tablespoon cornstarch
- 1 egg white
- Vegetable oil, for frying

For the Sauce:

- 2 tablespoons soy sauce
- 2 tablespoons hoisin sauce
- 1 tablespoon rice vinegar
- 1 tablespoon honey or brown sugar
- 1 teaspoon sesame oil
- 2 cloves garlic, minced
- 1 teaspoon minced ginger
- 1 teaspoon cornstarch mixed with 2 tablespoons water (for thickening)

Other Ingredients:

- 1 bell pepper, thinly sliced
- 1 onion, thinly sliced
- 2 green onions, chopped (for garnish)
- Toasted sesame seeds (for garnish)
- Cooked white rice, for serving

Instructions:

1. Marinate the Beef:
    1. In a bowl, combine thinly sliced beef with soy sauce, Shaoxing wine, sesame oil, cornstarch, and egg white. Mix well to coat the beef evenly. Let it marinate for at least 30 minutes, or refrigerate for up to 2 hours for best results.

2. Fry the Beef:

1. Heat vegetable oil in a wok or deep skillet over medium-high heat.
2. Once the oil is hot, carefully add the marinated beef slices in batches, ensuring they are not overcrowded. Fry for about 2-3 minutes until crispy and golden brown.
3. Remove the crispy beef from the oil using a slotted spoon and drain on paper towels. Repeat with the remaining beef slices.

3. Make the Sauce:
   1. In a small bowl, whisk together soy sauce, hoisin sauce, rice vinegar, honey or brown sugar, and sesame oil. Set aside.
   2. In the same wok or skillet, remove excess oil, leaving about 1 tablespoon behind.
   3. Add minced garlic and ginger to the wok and stir-fry for about 30 seconds until fragrant.
   4. Pour the sauce mixture into the wok and bring to a simmer.

4. Combine Beef and Sauce:
   1. Add the crispy beef back to the wok, along with thinly sliced bell pepper and onion. Toss everything together until the beef and vegetables are coated with the sauce.
   2. Cook for an additional 2-3 minutes until the sauce thickens and coats the beef and vegetables evenly.
   3. If the sauce is too thin, add the cornstarch-water mixture and stir until it thickens.

5. Garnish and Serve:
   1. Transfer the crispy shredded beef to a serving plate or bowl.
   2. Garnish with chopped green onions and toasted sesame seeds.
   3. Serve the crispy shredded beef immediately with steamed white rice.

6. Enjoy:
   1. Enjoy your homemade crispy shredded beef, savoring the crispy texture and flavorful sauce!

Feel free to customize this dish by adding other vegetables such as carrots, broccoli, or snap peas. Adjust the sweetness and saltiness of the sauce according to your taste preferences. Serve the crispy shredded beef as a delicious main dish for lunch or dinner, and enjoy the crispy texture paired with the tender beef and flavorful sauce.

Radish Cake (Luo Bo Gao)

Ingredients:

For the Radish Cake:

- 2 cups shredded radish (daikon radish)
- 1 cup rice flour
- 2 tablespoons cornstarch
- 1 1/2 cups water
- 2 Chinese sausages (lap cheong), diced
- 2-3 dried shiitake mushrooms, soaked and diced
- 2 tablespoons dried shrimp, soaked and chopped
- 2 tablespoons vegetable oil
- Salt, to taste
- White pepper, to taste

For Garnish:

- Chopped green onions
- Toasted sesame seeds
- Chili oil (optional)

Instructions:

1. Prepare the Radish Mixture:
    1. In a large bowl, combine shredded radish with a pinch of salt. Let it sit for about 10-15 minutes to release excess water.
    2. After 15 minutes, squeeze the excess water out of the shredded radish using your hands or a clean kitchen towel. Set aside.

2. Cook the Chinese Sausages and Mushrooms:
    1. Heat a skillet over medium heat. Add diced Chinese sausages and cook until they start to release oil and turn slightly crispy, about 2-3 minutes.
    2. Add diced shiitake mushrooms and chopped dried shrimp to the skillet. Cook for another 2-3 minutes until the mushrooms are tender. Remove from heat and set aside.

3. Make the Radish Cake Batter:

1. In a large mixing bowl, combine rice flour, cornstarch, and water. Stir until well combined and smooth.
2. Add the shredded radish, cooked Chinese sausages, mushrooms, and dried shrimp to the batter. Mix until evenly distributed.
3. Season the batter with salt and white pepper to taste.

4. Steam the Radish Cake:
    1. Grease a square or round cake pan with vegetable oil.
    2. Pour the radish cake batter into the greased cake pan, spreading it out evenly.
    3. Place the cake pan in a steamer basket or on a rack in a steamer.
    4. Steam the radish cake over high heat for about 40-50 minutes, or until it is firm and set.

5. Cool and Cut the Radish Cake:
    1. Remove the steamed radish cake from the steamer and let it cool for about 10-15 minutes.
    2. Once cooled, carefully unmold the radish cake onto a cutting board.
    3. Cut the radish cake into slices or cubes of your desired size.

6. Pan-Fry the Radish Cake:
    1. Heat a non-stick skillet or wok over medium heat. Add a little vegetable oil.
    2. Pan-fry the radish cake slices or cubes until they are golden brown and crispy on both sides, about 3-4 minutes per side.

7. Garnish and Serve:
    1. Transfer the crispy pan-fried radish cake to a serving plate.
    2. Garnish with chopped green onions and toasted sesame seeds.
    3. Serve hot with chili oil on the side for dipping, if desired.

8. Enjoy:
    1. Enjoy your homemade radish cake (Luo Bo Gao) as a delicious appetizer or side dish, savoring its crispy exterior and soft, savory interior!

Feel free to customize this recipe by adding other ingredients such as Chinese black fungus, dried scallops, or Chinese five-spice powder for added flavor. Serve the radish cake with your favorite dipping sauce or enjoy it on its own as a tasty snack or part of a dim sum feast.

Egg Custard Tarts (Dan Ta)

Ingredients:

For the Pastry:

- 1 1/4 cups all-purpose flour
- 1/4 cup powdered sugar
- 1/2 cup unsalted butter, cold and cubed
- 1 egg yolk
- 1-2 tablespoons ice water (as needed)

For the Custard Filling:

- 3/4 cup granulated sugar
- 1 cup water
- 1 cup evaporated milk
- 3 large eggs
- 1 teaspoon vanilla extract

Instructions:

1. Prepare the Pastry:

    1. In a large mixing bowl, combine the all-purpose flour and powdered sugar.
    2. Add the cold, cubed butter to the flour mixture. Use your fingers or a pastry cutter to rub the butter into the flour until it resembles coarse crumbs.
    3. Add the egg yolk and mix until the dough starts to come together. If the dough is too dry, add 1-2 tablespoons of ice water, a little at a time, until the dough forms a ball.
    4. Wrap the dough in plastic wrap and refrigerate for at least 30 minutes.

2. Make the Custard Filling:

    1. In a saucepan, combine granulated sugar and water. Heat over medium heat, stirring occasionally, until the sugar dissolves completely and the mixture comes to a simmer. Remove from heat and let it cool to room temperature.
    2. In a separate bowl, whisk together the evaporated milk, eggs, and vanilla extract until well combined.
    3. Gradually pour the cooled sugar syrup into the milk and egg mixture, whisking continuously until smooth.

3. Roll out the Pastry and Assemble the Tarts:

1. Preheat your oven to 375°F (190°C). Lightly grease a muffin tin or tart molds.
2. On a lightly floured surface, roll out the chilled pastry dough to about 1/8 inch thickness. Use a round cookie cutter or glass to cut out circles slightly larger than the diameter of your tart molds.
3. Press the pastry circles into the prepared tart molds, gently pressing the dough into the bottom and up the sides of the molds.
4. Trim off any excess dough hanging over the edges of the molds.

4. Fill the Tart Shells and Bake:

1. Pour the custard filling into the prepared tart shells, filling each one about 3/4 full.
2. Place the filled tart molds on a baking sheet and transfer to the preheated oven.
3. Bake for 20-25 minutes, or until the pastry is golden brown and the custard is set with a slight jiggle in the center.
4. Remove the tarts from the oven and let them cool in the molds for 5-10 minutes.

5. Serve and Enjoy:

1. Carefully remove the egg custard tarts from the molds and transfer them to a wire rack to cool completely.
2. Serve the tarts at room temperature or chilled, garnished with a sprinkle of powdered sugar if desired.
3. Enjoy your homemade egg custard tarts as a delightful treat for dessert or afternoon tea!

These egg custard tarts are best enjoyed fresh, but they can also be stored in an airtight container in the refrigerator for up to 3 days. Simply reheat them in the oven for a few minutes before serving, if desired.

www.ingramcontent.com/pod-product-compliance
Lightning Source LLC
LaVergne TN
LVHW081557060526
838201LV00054B/1942